Structure and Perversions

THE LACANIAN CLINICAL FIELD

A series of books edited by
Judith Feher Gurewich, Ph.D.
in collaboration with Susan Fairfield

Structure and Perversions

Joël Dor

TRANSLATED BY
Susan Fairfield

OTHER

Other Press
New York

STRUCTURE ET PERVERSIONS
© by Editions DENOEL 1987

STRUCTURE AND PERVERSIONS
Translation © 2001, Other Press, LLC

Production Editor: Robert D. Hack

This book was set in 11 pt. Berkeley by Alpha Graphics of Pittsfield, NH.

10 9 8 7 6 5 4 3 2 1

Library of Congress Cataloging-in-Publication Data

Dor, Joël.
    [Structure et perversions. English]
    Structure and perversions / Joël Dor ; translated by Susan Fairfield.
       p. cm.—(The Lacanian clinical field)
    Includes bibliographical references and index.
    ISBN 1-892746-37-9
    1. Psychoanalysis. 2. Lacan, Jacques, 1901- 3. Psychology, Pathological.
I. Title. II. Series.

RC506 .D64913 2001
616.89'17—dc21
                                             2001036424

This book is dedicated to M. D.
I am grateful to Françoise Bétourné
for her ongoing assistance throughout the writing process
and for her valuable help in editing.

"Perversion has a bad press. What first comes to mind is abnormal, deviant conduct, the indefensible manifestation of bad intentions, the criminal aberration that leads to perdition. The fact that the sonority of the word implies 'toward the father,' which will be the crux of this discussion, is most often concealed by the aura of scandal that accompanies it."

—René Tostain

Contents

The Lacanian Clinical Field: Series Overview

JUDITH FEHER GUREWICH

*L*acanian psychoanalysis exists, and the ongoing series, *The Lacanian Clinical Field*, is here to prove it. *The clinical expertise of French practitioners deeply influenced by the thought of Jacques Lacan has finally found a publishing home in the United States. Books that have been acclaimed in France, Italy, Spain, Greece, South America, and Japan for their clarity, didactic power, and clinical relevance will now be at the disposal of the American psychotherapeutic and academic communities. These books cover a range of topics, including theoretical introductions; clinical approaches to neurosis, perversion, and psychosis; child psychoanalysis; conceptualizations of femininity; psychoanalytic readings of American literature; and more. Thus far, the series is comprised of eleven titles.*

Though all these works are clinically relevant, they will also be of great interest to those American scholars who have taught and used Lacan's theories for over a decade. What better opportunity for the academic world of literary criticism, philosophy, human sciences, women's studies, film studies, and multicultural studies finally to have access to the clinical insights of a theorist known primarily for his revolutionary vision of the formation of the human subject. Thus The Lacanian Clinical Field goes beyond introducing the American clinician to a different psychoanalytic outlook. It brings together two communities that have grown progressively estranged from each other. For indeed, the time when the Frankfurt School, Lionel Trilling, Erich Fromm, Herbert Marcuse, Philip Rieff, and others were fostering exchanges between the academic and the psychoanalytic communities is gone, and in the process psychoanalysis has lost some of its vibrancy.

The very limited success of ego psychology in bringing psychoanalysis into the domain of science has left psychoanalysis in need of a metapsychology that is able not only to withstand the pernicious challenges of psychopharmacology and psychiatry but also to accommodate the findings of cognitive and developmental psychology. Infant research has put many of Freud's insights into question, and the attempts to replace a one-body psychology with a more interpersonal or intersubjective approach have led to dissension within the psychoanalytic community. Many theorists are of the opinion that the road toward scientific legitimacy requires a certain allegiance with Freud's detractors, who are convinced that the unconscious and its sexual underpinnings are merely an aberration. Psychoanalysis continues to be practiced, however, and according to both patients and analysts the uncovering of unconscious motivations continues to provide a sense of relief. But while there has been a burgeoning of different psychoanalytic schools of thought since the desacralization of Freud, no theoretical agreement has been reached as to why such relief occurs.

Nowadays it can sometimes seem that Freud is read much more scrupulously by literary critics and social scientists than by psychoanalysts. This is not entirely a coincidence. While the psychoanalytic community is searching for a new metapsychology, the human sciences have acquired a level of theoretical sophistication and complexity that has enabled them to read Freud under a new lens. Structural linguistics and structural anthropology have transformed conventional appraisals of human subjectivity and have given Freud's unconscious a new status. Lacan's teachings, along with the works of Foucault and Derrida, have been largely responsible for the explosion of new ideas that have enhanced the interdisciplinary movement pervasive in academia today.

The downside of this remarkable intellectual revolution, as far as psychoanalysis is concerned, is the fact that Lacan's contribution has been derailed from its original trajectory. No longer perceived as a theory meant to enlighten the practice of psychoanalysis, his brilliant formulations have been both adapted and criticized so as to conform to the needs of purely intellectual endeavors far removed from clinical reality. This state of affairs is certainly in part responsible for Lacan's dismissal by the psychoanalytic community. Moreover, Lacan's "impossible" style has been seen as yet another proof of the culture of obscurantism that French intellectuals seem so fond of.

In this context the works included in The Lacanian Clinical Field should serve as an eye-opener at both ends of the spectrum. The authors in the series are primarily clinicans eager to offer to professionals in psychoanalysis, psychiatry, psychology, and other mental-health disciplines a clear and succinct didactic view of Lacan's work. Their goal is not so much to emphasize the radically new insights of the Lacanian theory of subjectivity and its place in the history of human sciences as it is to show how this difficult and complex body of ideas can enhance clinical work. Therefore, while the American clinician will be made aware that Lacanian psychoanalysis is not primarily a staple of literary criticism or philosophy but a praxis meant to cure patients of their psychic distress, the academic community will be exposed for the first time to a reading of Lacan that is in sharp contrast with the literature that has thus far informed them about his theory. In that sense Lacan's teachings return to the clinical reality to which they primarily belong.

Moreover, the clinical approach of the books in this series will shed a new light on the critical amendments that literary scholars and femi-

nist theoreticians have brought to Lacan's conceptualization of subjectivity. While Lacan has been applauded for having offered an alternative to Freud's biological determinism, he has also been accused of
nevertheless remaining phallocentric in his formulation of sexual difference. Yet this criticism, one that may be valid outside of the clinical
reality—psychoanalysis is both an ingredient and an effect of culture—
may not have the same relevance in the clinical context. For psychoanalysis as a praxis has a radically different function from the one it
currently serves in academic discourse. In the latter, psychoanalysis is
perceived both as an ideology fostering patriarchal beliefs and as a theoretical tool for constructing a vision of the subject no longer dependent
on a phallocratic system. In the former, however, the issue of phallocracy
loses its political impact. Psychoanalytic practice can only retroactively
unravel the ways that the patient's psychic life has been constituted, and
in that sense it can only reveal the function the phallus plays in the psychic elaboration of sexual difference.

The Lacanian Clinical Field, therefore, aims to undo certain prejudices that have affected Lacan's reputation up to now in both the academic
and the psychoanalytic communities. While these prejudices stem from
rather different causes—Lacan is perceived as too patriarchal and reac-
tionary in the one and too far removed from clinical reality in the other—
they both seem to overlook the fact that the fifty years that cover the period of Lacan's teachings were mainly devoted to working and reworking
the meaning and function of psychoanalysis, not necessarily as a science
or even as a human science, but as a practice that can nonetheless rely on
a solid and coherent metapsychology. This double debunking of received
notions may not only enlarge the respective frames of reference of both
the therapeutic and the academic communities; it may also allow them to
find a common denominator in a metapsychology that has derived its "scientific" status from the unexpected realm of the humanities.

I would like to end this overview to the series as a whole with a
word of warning and a word of reassurance. One of the great difficul-

ties for an American analyst trying to figure out the Lacanian "genre" is the way these clinical theorists explain their theoretical point of view as if it were coming straight from Freud. Yet Lacan's Freud and the American Freud are far from being transparent to each other. Lacan dismantled the Freudian corpus and rebuilt it on entirely new foundations, so that the new edifice no longer resembled the old. At the same time he always downplayed, with a certain coquetterie, his position as a theory builder, because he was intent on proving that he had remained, despite all odds, true to Freud's deepest insights. Since Lacan was very insistent on keeping Freudian concepts as the raw material of his theory, Lacanian analysts of the second generation have followed in their master's footsteps and have continued to read Freud scrupulously in order to expand, with new insights, this large structure that had been laid out. Moreover, complicated historical circumstances have fostered their isolation, so that their acquaintance with recent psychoanalytic developments outside of France has been limited. Lacan's critical views on ego psychology and selected aspects of object relations theory have continued to inform their vision of American psychoanalysis and have left them unaware that certain of their misgivings about these schools of thought are shared by some of their colleagues in the United States. This apparently undying allegiance to Freud, therefore, does not necessarily mean that Lacanians have not moved beyond him, but rather that their approach is different from that of their American counterparts. While the latter often tend to situate their work as a reaction to Freud, the Lacanian strategy always consists in rescuing Freud's insights and resituating them in a context free of biological determinism.

Second, I want to repeat that the expository style of the books of this series bears no resemblance to Lacan's own writings. Lacan felt that Freud's clarity and didactic talent had ultimately led to distortions and oversimplifications, so that his own notoriously "impossible" style was meant to serve as a metaphor for the difficulty of listening to the unconscious. Cracking his difficult writings involves not only the intellectual effort of readers but also their unconscious processes; comprehension will dawn as reader-analysts recognize in their own work what was expressed in sibylline fashion in the text. Some of Lacan's followers continued this tradition, fearing that clear exposition would leave no room for the active participation of the reader. Others felt strongly that although Lacan's point was well taken it was not necessary to prolong indefinitely an ideology of obscurantism liable to fall into the same traps as the ones Lacan was denouncing in the first place. Such a conviction was precisely what made this series, The Lacanian Clinical Field, possible.

Introduction

The concept of "perversion" has been misused for a long time, corrupted in the everyday fare of the media. Whatever appeal it may have lies, at most, in its calling to mind some temptations ideologically designated as moral depravity, temptations that are the source of the power of attraction, indeed of fascination, commonly associated with perversion.

This brash seductiveness does not, however, seem to apply to perverse behavior, except under the strict condition that such behavior remain confined to what *other* people do. But there is no insult more self-deceiving than this imaginary defense on the part of the anonymous observer or commentator who experiences pleasure when someone else is deviating. For in fact, whether we admit it or not, perversion is something that applies to each of us, at least when it comes to the dynamics of desire that perversion expresses and that none of us can escape: "We can never say that the question of perversion does not concern us, since we are sure that, in any case, it concerns *us*" (Aulagnier 1967a, p. 79).

Does this amount to saying that we all consider ourselves to be affected in the same way as the pervert himself? Certainly not, as long as we are careful to define exactly what perversion is, beyond the ideological hodgepodge that surrounds it. But, conversely, getting our bearings in this way entails our being very precise about the "perverse core" that is to be found in all desire.

Only if this light is shed on the perverse process does it occupy a coherent and intelligible space both theoretically and clinically: the space of the psychosexual field. In this sense, there are no perversions other than sexual perversions, strictly speaking. This restriction is justified by the sole fact that perversions arise at the very heart of what Freud termed "so-called normal sexuality."

When we delimit the understanding of the perverse process in this way, we are ascribing to the perversions a structural identity that goes beyond the mere occurrence of a psychopathological scenario. Proof of this is the inadequacy of psychiatric expertise when it perpetuates the etiological myth of "constitutional perversions." If we are going to free the perversions from the ongoing influence of this sort of psychopathological reductionism, we have to clarify the problem of psychic structure and structural traits from the standpoint of diagnostic evaluation, that is, as we encounter them in clinical practice.

In order to make sense of the structural logic of the perverse process, we must also reexamine it from the very beginnings of Freudian thought. On the one hand we find, very generally speaking, the metapsychological mysteries that govern the instinctual course of psychic development up to the point at which, for each subject, the enigma of sexual difference must be resolved. On the other hand, and more precisely, we have to look at the conflicting desires of the oedipal entanglement. It is here that we find an anchoring point of the perversions in the phallic stakes that necessarily govern the course of this dialectic.

With a deeper investigation of this sort, it becomes possible to isolate certain structural traits that determine, rigorously and beyond any doubt, the specificity of the perverse structure. As a result, we can establish a clear differential distinction with respect to other symptomatic manifestations that might otherwise lead to diagnostic uncertainty in the area of clinical practice.

On the clinical level, while the metapsychological clarification of the perverse process also makes it easier to understand the close structural relationship of this process to certain types of psychopathological organization (psychoses and transsexualism), it nevertheless draws a line confirming the distinctive nature of the perversions. And it indirectly sheds light on the problem of the hypothetical existence of perversions in women.

*   *   *

Since I do not claim originality from the theoretical and clinical point of view, it seemed important, in taking up the issue of the perversions, to bring together a large amount of material that is often scattered in Freud's work and, all the more so, in the work of his followers. This manner of presentation should at least make for a certain coherence in approaching a psychic organization that never fails to cause trouble for the clinician as much for its underlying complexity as for the disturbing ways in which it manifests itself.

—Santa Lucia di Tallano
August 1986

Part I

Structure.
Structural Traits.
Diagnostic Assessment

1

The Notion of Diagnostic Assessment in Clinical Psychoanalysis

The problematics of the "diagnosis" of psychopathology deserve to be introduced by a return to the canon, to certain classical concepts set forth by Freud. Very early on, if not from the actual birth of psychoanalysis, Freud (1893–1895) raised the issue of diagnosis in the following terms:

> When I attempted to apply to a comparatively large number of patients Breuer's methods of treating hysterical symptoms by an investigation and abreaction of them under hypnosis, I came up against two difficulties, in the course of dealing with which I was led to an alteration both in my technique and in my view of the facts. (1) I found that not everyone could be hypnotized who exhibited undoubted hysterical symptoms and who, it was highly probable, was governed by the same psychical mechanism. (2) I was forced to take up a position

on the question of what, after all, essentially characterizes hysteria and what distinguishes it from other neuroses. [p. 256]

And he continues: "It is very hard to obtain a clear view of a case of neurosis before one has submitted it to a thorough analysis . . . ; *but a decision on the diagnosis and the form of therapy to be adopted has to be made before any thorough knowledge of the case has been arrived at*" (p. 256, emphasis added).

What this means is that, right on the threshold of his work, Freud revealed the ambiguity surrounding diagnosis in clinical psychoanalysis. On the one hand, he notes, it seems advisable to arrive at an early diagnosis so as to determine the treatment, or what nowadays we would call the conduct of the analysis. On the other hand, he hastens to explain that the accuracy of such a diagnosis can be confirmed only after an extended period.

Thus the specificity of a diagnosis clearly involves a paradox. How can we reconcile the pragmatic usefulness of a diagnosis with its relative provisionality? A detour into the domain of clinical medicine will enable us to clarify some aspects of the problems inherent in diagnosis.

In clinical medicine, diagnosis is above all an act that has two functions. First, it makes a semiological distinction, one that is based on the observation of certain signs. Second, it classifies the pathological state thus specified in terms of a codified nosography. A medical diagnosis, therefore, always has both etiological and differential referents. Moreover, it usually enables the physician to evaluate not only the vital or functional prognosis of the illness but the most appropriate course of treatment. To this end, the physician has at his disposal an arsenal of investigation that has two complementary orientations: investigation probing the patient's memory of the facts pertaining to the illness, and investigation centering on direct examination of the patient by instrumental, technical, biological, and other means. This twofold investigation gathers together the information needed for the precise identification of the pathological disturbance.

When it comes to clinical psychoanalysis, this kind of diagnostic determination is precluded. It is a de facto impossibility, since diagnosis depends on the very structure of the subject. The analyst has at his disposal only one investigative technique, and that is listening. No instrumental investigation can be undertaken. The clinical material brought in by the patient is essentially verbal, and so the field of clinical investigation is confined to the dimension of a *saying* and a *said* radically subject to the vicissitudes of the imaginary and the "lie": the imaginary, when speech surreptitiously articulates the way in which fantasy has been deployed; the lie, because the subject's speech reveals how blind he is to the truth of his desire. Hence the misunderstanding that promotes the disguise that is the symptom.

Since it is not based on objectively controllable empirical data, psychoanalytic diagnosis must be the result of an essentially subjective evaluation arrived at on the basis of the patient's discourse and the subjectivity of the listening analyst. Does this mean that, in the intersubjective field, there is no stable reference point? Are we limited to a space of purely empathic interactions? If that were the case, psychoanalytic investigation would be nothing more than a field of influence and suggestive strategies. Yet we know that psychoanalysis became a distinctive discipline only because Freud was able to separate the understanding of psychic processes from the domain of suggestion. We therefore have every reason to assume that it is legitimate to set forth a topography of psychopathological ailments.

Such a topography implies a set of reference points that can be arrived at only in terms of psychic causality and the accompanying, and unpredictable, processes that it sets in motion in the unconscious. Right from the beginning, then, the relation between a diagnosis and the choice of treatment does not depend on the usual logical causality that is obtained in clinical medicine. Let us recall the many reservations Freud (1913a) expressed in his study on beginning the treatment: "The extraordinary diversity of the psychical constellations concerned, the plasticity of all mental processes, and the wealth of determining factors oppose any mechanization of the technique; and they bring it about that a course of action that is as a rule justified may at times prove ineffective, whilst one that is usually mistaken may once in a while lead to the desired end" (p. 123). Yet Freud finds it necessary to add the following clarification: "These circumstances, however, do not prevent us from laying down a procedure . . . which is effective on the average" (p. 123).

From the perspective both of formulating the diagnosis and of directing the treatment that follows from it, the analyst is supposed to rely on stable elements despite the intersubjective dimension of the space in which this evaluation is conducted. But locating these stable elements calls for the greatest care. The orientation of the treatment depends on it, and so does its therapeutic success. Hence the danger of the "wild psychoanalysis" so firmly condemned by Freud. In a study devoted to this topic, Freud (1910) brilliantly illustrates not only the caution needed in establishing a diagnosis but the danger of any intervention based on the kind of objective causality found in medical diagnosis.

His clinical vignette involves a woman of about 50 who consults a young physician because of ongoing anxiety states. It seems to her that these anxiety attacks set in after her divorce. The young doctor, who has a smattering of psychoanalytic knowledge, immediately informs her of the cause of her anxiety in a terse explanation if there ever was one: the patient is suffering from the lack of any sexual relations with men. The therapy he suggests, therefore, is the logical implication of the cause of the ailment. If she is to get better, she has three possible courses of action. She can go back to her husband, take a lover, or masturbate! Obviously, this careless prescription has the expected effect: the woman's anxiety state gets worse, and this leads her to consult Freud.

Although it seems like a caricature, this brief example is instructive. It very neatly shows the difference between medical diagnosis and the kind of diagnosis that can be formulated in psychoanalysis. It also enables us to grasp the uniqueness of the connection between the diagnosis and the choice of treatment. In this vignette of Freud's, the diagnostic error is obvious. The issue is not so much to decide whether this young physician was familiar enough with the principles of psychoanalysis as it is to examine the way he went about his act of diagnosis.

Freud immediately observes that the doctor unwittingly made two mistakes. First, in his brusque prescription he rushed ahead of one of the essential factors in the therapeutic prognosis: the transference, a major element in the dynamics of an analytic intervention. Instead of making it his ally, he made it into an instrument of resistance. How, Freud protests, could the doctor have thought that a woman of this patient's age would not have known of the possibility of taking a lover, or did he overestimate his own influence to the point of believing that she would never take such a step without prior medical approval?

The doctor's second error involves the way in which a diagnosis is established. It is an excellent example of a procedure that has no place in clinical psychoanalysis, namely the hypothetico-deductive approach. In clinical psychoanalysis this procedure, governed as it is by the logical relation of cause and effect, cannot serve the purpose commonly assigned to it in the exact sciences. In the vignette the young, inexperienced therapist begins by establishing a connection between anxiety and sexual deprivation. In itself, such a connection is plausible, since we know, with Freud, that certain neurotic manifestations such as anxiety may well have to do with the "somatic sexual factor." It is clearly on this basis that the doctor quickly arrives at his diagnosis and suggests a therapy logically consistent with this causal relation.

The point is precisely to question the validity of the diagnosis here. In this case, the error is the result of the over-hasty causal reasoning that, in general, is the source of "wild" interpretation in psychoanalysis. Freud's comment is crystal clear in this regard:

> The lady who consulted the young doctor complained chiefly of anxiety states, and so he probably assumed that she was suffering from an anxiety neurosis and felt justified in recommending a somatic therapy to her. Again a convenient misapprehension! A person suffering from anxiety is not for that reason necessarily suffering from anxiety neurosis; such a diagnosis of it cannot be based on the name [of the symptom]. One has to know what signs constitute an anxiety neurosis and be able to distinguish it from other pathological states which are also manifested by anxiety. My impression was that the lady in question was suffering from anxiety hysteria, *and the whole value of such nosographical distinctions, one which quite justifies them, lies in the fact that they indicate a different aetiology and a different treatment.* No one who took into consideration the possibility of anxiety hysteria in this case would have fallen into the error of neglecting the mental factors, as this physician did with his three alternatives. [pp. 224–225, emphasis added]

Freud clearly formulates the problems of diagnostic ambiguity and caution, but he also emphasizes the direct relation between diagnostic assessment and the conduct of the treatment. Psychoanalytic action cannot automatically and logically follow from diagnostic identification. If it could, we would be similar to all medical disciplines in having treatises on analytic therapy at our disposal.

In the example mentioned by Freud, then, the primary technical error is assuming that the psychoanalytic act is like a medical one. Here again Freud's reservations are extremely valuable:

> It is a long superseded idea, and one derived from superficial appearances, that the patient suffers from a sort of ignorance, and that *if one removes this ignorance by giving him information (about the causal connection of the illness with his life, about his experiences in childhood, and so on)* he is bound to recover. The pathological factor is not his ignorance in itself, but the root of this ignorance is in his inner resistances; it was they that first called this ignorance into being, and they still maintain it now. . . . If knowledge about the unconscious were as important for the patient as people inexperienced in psychoanalysis imagine, listening to lectures or reading books would be enough to cure him. Such measures, however, have as much influence on the symptoms of nervous illness as a distribution of menu-cards in a time of famine has on hunger. . . . Psychoanalytic intervention, therefore, absolutely requires a fairly long period of contact with the patient. [pp. 224–225, emphasis added]

The same reservations are expressed in Freud's paper "On Beginning the Treatment" (1913a).

We are now in a position to draw several preliminary conclusions about psychoanalytic diagnosis. The first of these concerns its potential nature, that is, the fact that it is deliberately kept pending and open to a process of becoming. We have already noted this unique paradox: on the one hand, the near impossibility of making a diagnostic evaluation with assurance before the treatment has gone on for awhile, and on the other the need to have some sort of provisional diagnosis in order to determine the direction of the treatment. Diagnostic potentiality, open to confirmation in the future, thus suspends for a time any intervention of therapeutic value. This is a second conclusion that we can draw; a third, following from the first two, highlights the importance of taking the time to observe before making any decisions about the treatment. This time is what Freud at first called the trial period and is now known as the preliminary interviews. But, although this is a time of observation, it was part of analytic procedure right from the beginning. It is the only way to provide the proper conditions for a diagnostic assessment and a treatment plan.

Once again, let us note that Freud emphasized the need for analytic procedure right from the first sessions: "This preliminary experiment . . . is itself the beginning of a psycho-analysis and must conform to its rules. There may perhaps be this distinction made that in it one lets the patient do nearly all the talking and explains nothing more than what is absolutely necessary to get him to go on with what he is saying" (1913a, p. 124).

Diagnostic evaluation is thus primarily subject to the order of *saying*, more so than to the register of the *said* and its contents. In this sense, analytic procedure makes listening the foremost diagnostic instrument, one that takes precedence over nosographic information and causalist reasoning. These conclusions, drawn from the Freudian corpus, are illustrated in the work of Maud Mannoni (1965), who constantly emphasizes the immediate mobilization of the analyst's listening. The first interview, she says, reveals more through the distortions of speech than through its contents. And the many examples she offers are an excellent introduction to the problematics of diagnostic evaluation in clinical psychoanalysis.

2

Symptom and Diagnosis

In any medical practice, it is customary to set up correlations between the specificity of symptoms and a given diagnosis. Since the success of the therapeutic endeavor depends on them, fortunately such correlations are to be found most of the time. Yet a causalist arrangement works only because the body somehow responds to a way of functioning that itself obeys the same principle. The deeper the determinism, therefore, the larger the number of correlations between causes and effects and the more precise the specificity of the diagnosis.

Although this principle is uniformly accepted in all aspects of clinical medicine, it is grievously inadequate when it comes to analytic practice, on account of the unique determinism, known as psychic causality, that holds sway on the level of psychic processes. Psychic causality follows a different path from the usual chains of causes and effects familiar, for example, in the biological sciences.

The success of medical treatment is greatly dependent on the regularity and fixity of causal events taking place in the body. In contrast, although there is such a thing as psychic determinism, it is not possible to discern similar lines of regularity. In other words, no stable correlation between the nature of the causes and the nature of the effects can be ascertained with any degree of rigor. As a result, there can be no predictive profiles like those in the medical fields.

In science, a prediction is meaningful only because it is based on a law, that is, on an objective and generalizable explanation of a stable connection between causes and effects. Psychic causality obeys no such laws, at least not in the sense of the empirical and formal demands that define lawfulness in the exact sciences. In this situation—the absence of lawful connection between causes and effects and the resulting impossibility of reliable prediction—we must acknowledge that psychoanalysis is not a science in the strict acceptation of the term.

Let us take note of this first challenge: there is no stable inference between psychic causes and symptomatic effects. This invariable rule calls for attention, if only because it runs counter to our usual mental processes. Whether we acknowledge it or not, we think—indeed, we think of ourselves—in an order of Cartesian rationality. Thus we spontaneously tend to structure our explanations according to logical thought that is profoundly causalist in the sense of scientific discourse. Refusing this order of thought calls for an effort when psychoanalytic work is undertaken.

But the fact that it has to free itself from logical rationality does not mean that psychoanalytic work is left open to everybody's whim. Not all things are possible, and the work remains bound by certain demands for rigor, at least those that enjoin us to follow the thread of the utterance of the person we are listening to, if we want to be sure to find something of the structure of the subject on which to base a diagnostic evaluation.

In assuming that we can validate a diagnostic hypothesis by referring to concrete symptoms, we are implicitly admitting an irreducible relation of cause and effect. As we shall see, this amounts to completely ignoring the dynamics proper to the unconscious. Clinical practice teaches us that the relation between the symptom and its cause is mediated by a set of unconscious processes. The connection between a symptom and a diagnosis presupposes, at a minimum, the enactment of a chain of intrapsychic processes whose dynamics are not subject to ordinary causal determination.

Any of the mechanisms of the primary process will offer us irrefutable proof of this disconcerting logic of the unconscious. Let us take as an example the particular drive vicissitude that Freud (1915) calls turning against the self:

> The turning round of an instinct upon the subject's own self is made plausible by the reflection that masochism is actually sadism turned round upon the subject's own ego, and that exhibitionism includes looking at his own body. Analytic observation, indeed, leaves us in no doubt that the masochist shares in the enjoyment of the assault upon himself, and that the exhibitionist shares in the enjoyment of [the sight of] his exposure. [p. 127]

If a symptomatic act like sadism presupposes this contradictory logic of turning against the self, the very nature of the process described by Freud automatically invalidates the idea of a direct causal relation between a symptom and a diagnosis.

This first argument has to be taken further. Let us suppose that this contradictory logic is stable on the level of unconscious processes. In that case, we could consider the opposite pairs sadism / masochism and exhibitionism / voyeurism to be fixed equivalents. But even here we are not always able to infer a reliable diagnosis on the basis of symptoms. If we assume that symp-

tomatic activity of a voyeuristic nature logically implies exhibitionism (that is, that the reversal into the opposite is a fixed law), can
we logically arrive at a diagnosis of perversion given a symptom
like exhibitionism? Once again, the data of everyday clinical experience invalidate such an immediate conclusion. For example, an
element of exhibitionism is often prominent in hysteria, in the
sometimes very spectacular way in which the hysteric "shows off."

We need similar reserve clauses in another scenario, the symptomatic activity of orderliness and tidiness. In certain subjects, this
symptom extends to the point where it arouses anxiety and becomes
a true disability with regard to action. In the Freudian tradition
(1908b, 1913b, 1917) this character trait, which often reaches symptomatic proportions, is ascribed to the anal-erotic component of obsessional neurosis. Given this symptom alone, could we make a
diagnosis of obsessional neurosis? Not any more than in the preceding case, for the simple reason that this symptom, too, also occurs
in a very active form in hysteria. In fact, it is especially florid in certain hysterical women when it comes to housekeeping. Most often
it is a symptom of borrowing from the spouse; in her readiness to
identify with the desire of the other, the hysteric readily takes on
the symptom of her obsessional partner.

There is, then, no direct overlap between a cartography of
symptoms and a diagnostic classification. This discontinuity forces
us to recenter the problem in the light of unconscious processes,
which can never be observed directly. And it is because direct
observation is not possible that the patient's active participation is
called for. In the domain of psychoanalysis, this participation takes
the form of speech. Here we find the Freudian prescription that is
at the forefront of psychoanalysis: if the dream is the royal road to
the unconscious, it is so only because the subject gives a verbal
account of his dream. Strictly speaking, then, the royal road is

discourse itself. The enactments of unconscious processes cannot be decoded with the tools of explanatory, deductive reasoning in the manner of a pseudo-science, but exclusively through the patient's verbal associations.

In his "return to Freud," Lacan repeatedly insisted on the primacy of discourse in psychoanalysis, as for example in "The Agency of the Letter in the Unconscious or Reason Since Freud": "And how could a psychoanalyst of today not realize that speech is the key to that truth, when his whole experience must find in speech alone its instrument, its context, its material, and even the background noise of its uncertainties? . . . As my title suggests, beyond this 'speech,' what psychoanalytic experience discovers in the unconscious is the whole structure of language" (1957a, p. 147).

Lacan's emphasis on the impact of speech in the experience of the unconscious is also to be found in his paper on "The Situation of Psychoanalysis in 1956":

> To know what is happening in the analysis, we have to know where speech is coming from. To know what the resistance is, we have to know what is preventing speech from coming to the fore. . . .
>
> Why elude the questions that the unconscious provokes?
>
> If so-called free association gives us access to it, is it through a liberation comparable to those of neurological reflexes?
>
> If the drives discovered there are on the diencephalic level, or even the rhinencephalic, how can we conceive that they are structured in terms of language?
>
> For if, from the beginning, it is in language that their effects become known, their ruses that we have subsequently learned to recognize, they do not denote any the less, in their triviality as well as in their refinements, a linguistic procedure. [1956, pp. 461–466]

To return more directly to the problematics of the symptom, let us also recall this brief formulation from the Rome discourse: "[T]he symptom resolves itself entirely in an analysis of language, because the symptom is itself structured like a language, because it is from language that speech must be delivered" (1953, p. 59). If the symptom comes under the heading of speech and language, it seems clear that diagnosis must do so as well, that what we call *structural diagnostic reference points* are to be assigned to the register of speech. In any event, they will not constitute reliable elements in diagnostic evaluation unless they are removed from the category of the identification of symptoms. The identity of a symptom is most often a smokescreen, an artifact of the effects of the unconscious that Lacan, echoing Freud, calls its ruses and tricks.

Diagnostic investigation must find support on the "near side" of the symptom, in that intersubjective space in which Freud, in his famous telephone metaphor, described the communication of one unconscious to another:

> [The analyst] must turn his own unconscious like a receptive organ towards the transmitting unconscious of the patient. He must adjust himself to the patient as a telephone receiver is adjusted to the transmitting microphone. Just as the receiver converts back into sound-waves the electric oscillations in the telephone line which were set up by sound-waves, so the doctor's unconscious is able, from the derivatives of the unconscious which are communicated to him, to reconstruct that unconscious, which has determined the patient's free associations. [1912, p. 116]

Structural diagnostic reference points appear in the deployment of speech, in the form of signifying breakthroughs of desire that are taking shape in the speaker. Thus these reference points are indicators of the psychic structure itself. They somehow represent signposts set up by the dynamics of desire. As we shall see, a subject's specific structure is predetermined by the economy of his desire. Now, this economy is governed by fixed orientations and trajectories and hence by certain traffic rules, as it were. If such stable trajectories may be called *structural traits*, structural diagnostic reference points are signs coded by these traits that bear witness to the economy of desire.

In order to get a better understanding of the operative nature of diagnosis, it is important to clarify the notion of structure and the distinction between symptoms and structural traits.

3

The Distinction between Symptoms and Structural Traits. Illustration in a Case of Hysteria

PRELIMINARY INTERVIEWS

Appropriate use of diagnosis in the field of clinical psychoanalysis presupposes a rigorous and ongoing differentiation between the symptom and structural traits. Without such continuous vigilance, the clinician runs the risk of making major diagnostic errors that can seriously compromise the therapeutic prognosis. The clinical case to be discussed is a prime example of this type of confusion.[1] From the very first sessions of this treatment, it is clear that there is a radical distinction between the determina-

---

1. The amnestic details presented here have been detached from their intricate psychopathological context. The history of this patient—who has since died accidentally—will be presented only to the extent necessary for the illustration of the technical issue we are considering.

tion of certain structural characteristics and the spectacular nature of the symptom.

The First Session

Ms. X., a single woman of barely 30 years of age, was referred to me by an internist upon leaving the hospital. In the initial interview, this stay in the hospital was her major piece of information, mentioned to me abruptly but with no account of the reason behind it. Yet although nothing was said directly about it, in the course of the interview I was able to observe clear evidence of a structural trait, in this case a characteristic feature of hysterical structure.

This young woman complained of a vague but quite pervasive malaise, though she was unable to associate its manifestations with any particular situations. Nothing escaped it, and both her everyday personal life and her career were affected. In brief, she explained that she took no interest in anything: in projects, or in any sort of relationships with other people, close or not. Both people and things bored her profoundly and were quickly dropped. Against this background of depression and despondency she spent most of her time doing nothing, apart from brooding without much pleasure during the day.

Nevertheless, amid these confused daydreams a fantasy theme often recurred in an obsessive-compulsive manner. In this imaginary scenario that she regularly called to mind, a male friend would pay her an unexpected visit one evening. This visit would be disconcerting, yet pleasantly so. Caught by surprise in an unkempt state, she would settle her friend comfortably and then retire for a moment to the bathroom in order to make herself more presentable. The fantasy scenario would always proceed in the following manner. Alone in the bathroom, she would enjoy imagining, with a delight she could not explain, what her friend might think she was doing in there. And yet, she explained, it was very strange that—to her great displeasure and despite her repeated efforts to keep it going—the fantasy always came to a stop at that point.

After she had described this fantasy, I asked, "What were you thinking about on the other side of my office door, in the waiting room?" My intervention immediately evoked a reaction entirely characteristic of hysterical functioning: a repression immediately associated with a displacement. The patient said she was feeling too warm, took off her jacket, and revealed forearms disfigured by the traces of scars, some of which were recent and still painted with iodine. Upon her showing me these injuries, I broke off the session.

Concise as they are, these few bits of material brought into the first interview already suggest some important things to keep in mind with regard to the distinction to be made between structural features and symptoms.

From the outset, this patient presenting with an underlying depression revealed a structural diagnostic landmark corresponding to a trait of hysterical structure. After immediately informing me that she had just left the hospital, this woman said nothing further about it and began to talk of other matters. It was as though everything had been implicitly made known in this brief communication, even though nothing had been clearly spelled out. In other words, she conveyed something to me in such a manner that I had to guess at it and ask her about it. This kind of intersubjective functioning presupposes a strategy of desire characteristic of hysterical structure: desiring something by having to make it be desired by the other. In a certain way, then, her desire became the object of my own demand.

If the hysteric is always there without really being there (which is what we call the hysterical pretense), this is so because of a remarkable feature of hysterical structure: the subject's desire is always there, but only provided it gets itself represented where it is not by finding a proxy in the desire of the other.

Telling the difference between a structural trait and a symptom depends on spotting such indications. Beyond the plasticity and the diversity of symptoms, the structural trait makes its presence felt as a stable element that announces a strategy of desire. We can highlight this characteristic feature of hysteria with reference to the process of repression and displacement as it was revealed in the structure of the fantasy scenario and actualized following my intervention.

If fantasy is always nothing but a scenario of desire, we should be able to identify a corresponding profile of the strategy of desire. The patient's fantasy brought a man on stage. But this imaginary elaboration did not introduce him at random. The man always arrived unexpectedly. He appeared on the scene only in order to mobilize this woman's desire in an unforeseeable way. Furthermore, the unfolding of the fantasy shows that this mobilization of desire remained suspended at the query: "What does he want of me?" Since the scenario was completely private, it served only to express the subject's chosen personal economy of desire, which functioned through representation in the desire of the other. It is because the "other" of the fantasy was assumed to desire something in her place that the patient was able to locate herself in a situation of desire.

The rest of the scenario constituted a significant response to this mobilization of desire. She disappeared into the bathroom under the pretext of making herself more presentable. Here we have an essential characteristic of hysteria, the function of the mask. With the mask, the hysteric places herself at a distance from herself and thus from her desire, so that she may remain in ignorance of this desire. The logical sequence of the fantasy unfolds: having retreated into the bathroom, she took pleasure in figuring out what the other imagined her to be doing there. Here we can identify the strategy of desire, interrogating the desire of the other with the sole aim of knowing what one's own is like, as well as the paradigm of alienation of the subject's desire through the desire of the other.

The abrupt ending of the fantasy scenario, too, can be accurately explained as an expression of this structural trait. The fantasy always broke off at this point of alienation, thereby actualizing the suspension of desire characteristic of the hysterical position. Corresponding to this placing of desire in suspension were some standard symptomatic expressions whose preferred formulas are of the type: "I don't want anything," "nothing interests me," "nothing makes any difference to me," and the like. This is a perfect example of the discrepancy between the structural trait and the symptom. The symptom is a product of psychic elaboration, an offshoot of structure whose nature provides no particular diagnostic guarantee. It can even on occasion serve to disrupt the process of identifying structural traits.

To return to the analysis of the session: when I intervened, I punctuated the evocation of the fantasy scenario, focusing the question of this patient's desire back to the only place in which it arises, namely, in herself and not in the desire of the other.

Since waiting behind my office door was clearly a metaphor for the structure of her favorite fantasy, my intervention aimed solely at reversing its modality. The reverse of the fantasy scenario in which she asked herself about the other's desire was, now, the other asking her what she had been thinking about as she waited. Such an intervention recenters the locus in which desire arises, selectively defusing the hysterical dynamic, because it occurs as an intrusion equivalent to the query: "From what place do you desire?" The response to my question was all I needed to confirm the presence of this hysterical dynamic quite exactly— first, repression: "It's hot in here," she said, taking off her jacket, and then displacement onto the "body symptom," the revealing of her wounded, bruised forearms.

The patient's response to my metaphoric intervention, "From what place do you desire?" could only take the form of a blind neurotic logic as she showed me something about her body, exhibiting the symptom fragment in which her desire was in fact held captive. She did, indeed, desire in her body at the level of the mutilated forearms that she revealed to my attention. In so doing, she demonstrated the favorite path taken by hysterical desire, which chooses a suffering body part.

My reply to this was to return the question of desire to the place where it belonged, instead of leaving it in the place where it had been alienated. I refused to look and asked her to cover herself back up, ending the session.

The Second Session

The following session opened with an unusual comment: "I won't shake hands; I'm in treatment and wouldn't want to infect you." Besides the fact that this warning could be understood as a radical denial, its essential interest lay in its being the opening move in a strategy of intrigue aimed, once again, at actualizing a metaphor of the body symptom.

Although my attention could be aroused on the level of a privileged body fragment (the hand), it was in quite a different place that the veil was, so to speak, lifted. Thanks to a very short skirt and appropriate maneuvering of her legs, this woman let me see, as she sat down, scars from self-mutilation on her thighs identical to those on her forearms (which, that day, were completely covered). This scenario revealed the same structural feature noted before: the arousal of the other's attention in order to make him want to ask her what she herself wanted to let him know.

My intervention this time took a different form. I asked her whether she knew the following Jewish story: "Two Jews met in a railway carriage at a station in Galicia. 'Where are you going?' asked one. 'To Cracow,' was the answer. 'What a liar you are!' broke out the other. 'If you say you're going to Cracow, you want me to believe you're going to Lemberg. But I know that in fact you're going to Cracow. So why are you lying to me?'" (Freud 1905a, p. 115).

The unexpected introduction of this narrative in the session produced an entirely characteristic reaction. The young woman immediately stopped exhibiting her legs in apparent innocence. She associated to a fragment of speech, in the course of which I learned that, in the presence of someone else, she often felt boring, trivial, without anything interesting to say. This impromptu remark gave me the opportunity to observe to her that this was probably why she made her body speak instead.

I finally got a full account of her mutilated body, far surpassing what she had shown me. I learned that not only her arms and legs, but also her stomach and breasts had been cut in the same fashion. I was also told of her stay in the hospital, where she had just been treated for a widespread infection following from her repeated self-mutilation. This was, moreover, the sixth such hospitalization. Indeed, from the age of 17 onward she had continually mutilated herself, but without understanding the reasons for this morbid impulse that always arose uncontrollably and according to a standard pattern.

The self-mutilation initially appeared in the wake of an incident that remained perfectly incomprehensible and without any apparent logical connection to this symptom. When she was 17, she was suddenly overcome with anxiety during a class at high school. Unable to say a word, she could not help urinating and lost consciousness immediately afterwards. The indisposition lasted a few minutes and then, so it seemed, she felt fine again. Arriving home several hours later, she rushed into the bathroom and, after getting completely undressed, slashed her right breast with a razor blade. She was in a state of dissociation and felt no pain. On the contrary, when the blood began to flow she felt an unaccustomed effect of well being that lasted until the end of this brief hemorrhage. Totally exhausted, she took a bath and lay down to sleep for many hours.

Since that time, the symptom had been repeated according to an invariable scenario, on some days several times but on different parts of her body. In addition to the hospitalizations due to serious infectious syndromes, the patient also mentioned several stays in "rest homes." She later confided that these were, in reality, psychiatric clinics in which she had been hospitalized on various occasions with a diagnosis of schizophrenia.

Two interviews were necessary for this symptom to take the form of a narrative articulating its origin and repetition, but a full year of treatment passed before it collapsed and yielded up a meaning that had been overdetermined by an astonishing hysterical dynamic. A further few months made it possible to clarify the specific "choice" of self-mutilation as her mode of organization.

THE TREATMENT

The account of the very thorough analytic work carried out by this patient during her treatment would be of little interest were it not for the fact that it reveals the synergy of processes that happened to become involved in the remarkable construction of a symptom. This intrapsychic dynamic—even if merely reconstructed in a case report—well illustrates the disparity between the stability of the symptom and the primacy of the structural traits. This case example is also a model illustration because it is not often that a patient manages to recall with such a high degree of clarity and rigor the elements contributing to the formation of her symptom. (Needless to say, it was only in retrospect that the determining factors were identified.)

These different elements were either fantasy constructions or memories, some of the latter, formerly repressed, returning in the dynamics of the treatment. The first such decisive factor was a memory of an episode that had been completely forgotten but was quickly recalled at the beginning of our work. This was a rather unusual scene, accidentally observed by the patient when she was about 15. Along with other young people of her age, she was taking part in a skiing program. One evening she left her room and went to the reception desk of the hotel to make a phone call. She found no one there, but she heard laughter and shouting coming from the pantry. She couldn't help looking through the keyhole, where she witnessed a strange game being played by a female skiing instructor and several male instructors. The woman, in a ski outfit, was blindfolded. The men took turns walking around her while spraying her with whipped cream from an aerosol can that they passed from one to another. Worried about being caught spying, the patient quickly returned to her room.

Oddly enough, the adolescent remembered only one disturbing detail of this scene, the woman instructor's tight-fitting red ski outfit down which whipped cream was dripping. On the surface, at any rate, she was completely unaware of the obviously sexual connotation of the game.

Here we find one of the characteristic features of hysterical structure that was mentioned earlier, the combined process of repression and displacement. While the girl was obviously aroused by the sexual metaphor of the game, she immediately repressed the sexual connotation in favor of fixation on a feature that later turned out to be an identificatory trait. This is a perfect example of the process described by Freud (1921) as identification with a single trait, or what Lacan calls identification with the unary trait. This type of identification has a special place in hysteria.

The return of this memory led to further important associations with regard to the skiing program. Three episodes, apparently innocent and without logical connection to each other, were recalled in this way. First, the patient remembered the unaccustomed pleasure she experienced, during her stay, while taking frequent showers in the course of which she would let water flow over her body for a long time. She also recalled the inexplicable empathic connection she had felt with the woman instructor throughout the duration of the program. This was, of course, an unconscious identification manifesting itself as a well-known structural trait.

The third memory, which emerged later, differed from the two earlier ones in that it was directly sexual. When she awoke one morning she caught her roommate, a student teacher, fondling her breasts with evident pleasure in front of the mirror. Somewhat taken aback by her companion's boldness, she made believe she was still asleep and waited for the other girl to stop.

It took the full course of the treatment and the dynamics of the transference to bring out the true role of these various elements, which had been forgotten as events without importance but were in fact crucial to the symptomatic process.

Afterwards another key memory returned during a session. While at home one evening, watching television, the patient had been seized by a fit of laughter so uncontrollable that, as she distinctly recalled, she had passed some urine. Strangely enough, it was not until several sessions later that she was able to give some content to this episode by remembering the television show. It had involved a magician who mimed the ritual of the Catholic mass. Pouring some wine from a flask into a communion cup, this "comedian" drank it down, pretended to choke, and, with a mighty belch, coughed up a thermometer.

Yet another important event was recalled, several months later, in the interval between two sessions. The patient had been about 16 years old. Changing into her bathing suit in a pool cabana, she heard a man's voice addressing her on the other side of the door: "If you want to make love, come to the dressing room!" Opening the door a few seconds later, she saw no one. The situation was so surprising that for a moment she thought she had hallucinated the voice, but awhile later, leaving the pool area, she was very reassured when she found a blond woman in the dressing room. Afterwards, when she returned to the pool on several occasions, she imagined the same scenario. But the self-satisfied delight she took in this fantasy always ended with a hint of disappointment that the fantasy was never fulfilled.

About one year into the treatment, another memory decisively altered the course of the analytic work. It was as if the series of events to which it referred had crystallized, in an unconscious signifying logic, the already overdetermined material of the previous recollections.

This memory concerned a scene in which she had been the protagonist some time before the onset of the self-mutilation. She had not exactly forgotten this scene, but her memory of it was that of a reconstructed event. It took several sessions before she managed to articulate it with any precision. Originally, she recalled the episode in the following manner. She was at a party at the house of a 20-year-old female friend. During the evening, after she had been dancing, she headed toward the bathroom in order to fix her makeup and hair. The door was closed, but she sensed that an argument was going on in there between a man and a woman who were exchanging heated remarks. She believed she could identify the voice of her friend. Gripped by this unexpected turn of events, she stood dumbfounded, hearing nothing, fixed to the spot, and racked by abdominal spasms. After a few seconds her distress eased up and she was able to walk away.

Later on some important details were added to this memory. Not only was the woman crying or moaning, but the man with her kept urging her to be quiet: "Not so loud!" or "Not too loud!" ("*Pas trop fort!*") These were the words that seem to have caused her distress and her abdominal spasms. But while she fleetingly thought that the couple were making love, she at once persuaded herself that what was taking place was just a quarrel. As for the spasms, she realized in retrospect that she had probably had an orgasm, something she had apparently not experienced before.

This was a crucial point in the treatment. Detailed associative investigation revealed how certain signifiers had been selectively elaborated by the unconscious in a combination of successive metaphoric and metonymic substitutions that crystallized the pathological symptom of self-mutilation.

As we shall see, the hidden activity of the unconscious in the case of this patient illustrates the difference between a structural trait and a symptom. Though the symptom in its sheer presence is by nature purely contingent, there is nonetheless a certain necessity in the unconscious processes that work to produce it. To say that the nature of the symptom is relatively indiscriminate is to acknowledge that there is no logically necessary connection between the form that the symptom takes and the expression of the desire that is alienated in it. On the other hand, the strategies unconsciously utilized by the subject in the construction of the symptom are never indiscriminate. These strategies conform to a structure. More precisely, structural traits can be identified on the basis of this strategic elaboration.

We know that the symptom is primarily a form of wish-fulfillment.[2] How does a specific structure make use of signifying material to fulfill an unconscious desire? In this patient the fulfillment of desire brought about two remarkable unconscious formations: an obsessional fantasy and a symptom of self-mutilation. And we may also note, in the patient's signifying material, various structural traits that mobilized strategies characteristic of this case of hysteria.

The first two signifying elements that happened to become involved in the construction of the symptom were the very form-fitting red ski outfit and the whipped cream sprayed by the men onto a woman's body. The scene in which these two elements appeared was immediately experienced as a metaphor of sexual pleasure. For this reason it was at once repressed as far as its sexual import was concerned. At most, what remained was the playfulness and oddity of the episode: some men were having a good time joking around in a kitchen with a woman in a ski outfit.

In this process we can identify a characteristic operation of hysterical structure: the neutralization of sexual affect by means of repression and displacement. This displacement usually works in the direction of utter triviality. In addition, we have here another component of the hysterical problematic: the reversal of sexual affects. While hysterical subjects tend to reduce to triviality what has registered as a genuinely sexual situation, they are also incredibly good at erotizing a situation that is not, at first sight, sexual. These alternatives, all but inevitable in the economy of hysterical structure, can be explained by the mode of inscription specific to hysteria with regard to the phallic function. We can

---

2. Translator's note: the text has *accomplissement de désir*. In the French psychoanalytic tradition, *désir* ("desire") is used to translate Freud's *Wunsch* ("wish"), and I shall use "desire" in what follows.

therefore identify a structural trait in this process, above and beyond any symptom. In this case the kitchen episode was radically desexualized, but the charge of erotic affect nevertheless persisted, unconsciously linked to certain signifying elements. The very tight ski outfit thus constituted the signifier of the naked body uncovered in front of men and offered as metaphorical support for the sperm signified by the whipped cream. The scene was inscribed in its unconscious sexual connotation around these signifiers. As such, it could continue to mobilize the subject's repressed sexual excitement.

And so it is not very surprising to note that, afterwards, the patient found herself taking pleasure in a new experience: she would let water flow over her body for a long time when she was in the shower. We have here the second aspect of the hysterical trait mentioned above, the process of displacement. But we have to be precise about this process if we are to understand its typically hysterical component. As a result of displacement, it was from now on the subject who enjoyed making something stream over her nude body. This presupposes the carrying out of an unconscious identification—here, with the woman ski instructor who had seemed to take great pleasure in her game with the men. In the present case, the displacement was promoted by an identification with a unary trait. For this reason, and for this reason alone, the repression / displacement unquestionably reveals a structural trait. In other structures, the mechanism of repression / displacement is not necessarily set in motion by an identificatory process. Here, the woman instructor became for the moment an object of empathy, although the patient could not explain why; the instructor was, on the unconscious level, the patient herself experiencing sexual pleasure.

On this level we can already understand how selected signifiers are associated with one another and form a chain that, outside the subject's awareness, brings about a new meaning. The association of "ski outfit / naked body" and "whipped cream / sperm" helped to transform the flowing of water over the body into a signifying condensation representing intercourse with a man. The signifier "bathroom / toilet" also played an important role in this signifying association. It became the signifier of the place where this woman could henceforth have a metaphorical orgasm with a man while taking a shower.

In one of the other scenes mentioned earlier we can locate the signifiers in the same way. When the patient caught her room-mate fondling her breasts, a new unconscious inscription was established. From the time that one woman took her solitary pleasure, assuming that the other was asleep, the signifier "breast" telescoped the chain of prior signifiers. The breast was inscribed as the signifier not only of a possible pleasure but also of a pleasure that a woman can obtain for herself without a man. Moreover, it also became associated with the special connotation of taking pleasure without being seen. We can therefore assume that, from then on, a signifying selection was carried out to inscribe the boundary of intimate pleasure.

Sleep functions here as a screen concealing one woman's pleasure with regard to another. This screen signifier retroactively echoes the content of earlier scenes. We find it again in the pantry door behind which the ski instructor was enjoying herself in the company of men, and in the bathroom door behind which the patient took cover in order to reach the same goal metaphorically.

In the next scene, the television show, several other signifiers came to be associated unconsciously in a way that proved decisive. The television sequence had three phases: the communion wine was drunk, the magician choked, he coughed up a thermometer. In this stand-up comedian's routine there was, first, the selection of the signifier "red" (the color of the communion wine).

To this was associated, by way of condensation, the signifier of the erect penis, metaphorically represented by the thermometer coming out of the man's mouth.

The constitution of the chain of unconscious signifiers was completed in the following way. The signifier of the erection was from then on associated with the signifier "red," because it metonymically echoed the signifier of the body of the woman in the red outfit who was experiencing pleasure. "Red" thus became an unconscious metaphor for having sexual pleasure with a man and was, furthermore, associated with the experience of something streaming down the body. As for the fit of irrepressible laughter, it is the signifying metaphor of desire and the upsurge of the orgasm whose culmination was expressed by that other signifying metaphor of uncontrollable urination. Once again we find the mechanism of repression / displacement at work.

The scene at the pool was also the occasion of several unconscious signifying condensations of the same type. It took place in a cabana where she was getting undressed, that is, in an enclosed area where she was protected from the man who was propositioning her. The screen signifier was again put into operation around sexual pleasure, except that it was now explicitly linked to the signifier of making love with a man. These three signifiers were to become associated with each other through the affect that marked the end of the episode. Why did the patient feel so reassured when she saw a woman in the dressing room when she left the pool? For a brief moment she identified unconsciously with this woman, who like her was a blonde. It was as if she, the patient, were already at the place where the man had invited her to come in order to make love. Here again is the process of identification with a single trait—in this case the hair color—supporting an unconscious sexual metaphorization.

Let us now look at the last memory that organized the set of unconscious signifiers so as to precipitate the symptom. In this episode, her friend's love scene in the bathroom, the signifier "not so loud" or "not too loud" ("*pas trop fort*") catalyzed the signifying material into a final metaphorization of having sex with a man. An additional element also played a crucial role here. While the patient was an auditory witness to an event she was unable to see, she heard nothing.[3] This "hearing nothing" appeared after the fact, as evidence of her unconscious identification with the woman whom she supposed to be experiencing sexual pleasure. Completely identified with her friend at that moment, she wished that, in similar circumstances, she herself would not be able to be overheard by anyone outside the room. Under the influence of this screen signifier, there occurred a displacement between the two terms of a signifying oscillation: the "hearing nothing" turned into "without being heard," which in turn was the metonymic echo of the "without being seen" in the earlier sequences. In the course of this episode, still other signifying series were evoked by means of identity or metonymic proximity. In addition to the signifier "bathroom / toilet," there was the signifying reference to a man's voice coming from behind a door. And it was because this signifier was already unconsciously associated with the sex act that the first thought that came into her mind—however fleetingly—was precisely that, although this thought was then rejected in favor of the fantasy that a quarrel was taking place.

It is important to note that this episode involved the first occurrence of the signifier of pain and suffering, a signifier that turned out to be essential in the structuring of the symptom. The idea of having sex with a man, though repressed, was nonethe-

---

3. Translator's note: there is a pun here on the double meaning of *entendre*, "to hear" and "to understand."

less associated in fantasy not only with violence but also with pain. The conclusion of this sequence clearly reveals this unconscious association between sexual pleasure and physical suffering: her first orgasm could be registered only through bodily pain, in the metaphor of abdominal spasms.

Thus little by little a community of signifiers was separated out that, in the play of metaphoric and / or metonymic connections, called forth still other signifiers. Yet while this chain was constituted by a variety of different signifiers, their mutual combining always took place according to similar processes. These processes, therefore, may be identified as salient features of the hysterical structure.

Although it is incoherent, this chain of repressed signifiers nevertheless metaphorically represents the fulfillment of desire. The repressed signifying elements still have to undergo one last modification before they irrupt into the subject's awareness in such a way that the fulfillment of desire is revealed in a completely unrecognizable form. In other words, this signifying organization must be able to be disguised in a synthetic form of expression—in the present case an unconscious formation crystallized in a symptom of self-mutilation.

To this end, the unconscious material underwent a final elaboration, thanks to a precipitating event. This event functioned as a sort of catalyst promoting the chemical reaction of several substances with one another, but without adding anything to the composition of the new chemical substance that resulted. In this case, the new chemical substance was the emergence of the symptom, and the catalyst was the following event from the patient's school days. She took some time to recall this episode.

During a class in physical chemistry, the instructor was commenting on the procedure of an experiment he was performing before his students. The patient remembered a test tube filled with a chemical solution colored red, which he carefully poured into an evaporating dish where a precipitate boiled up. Although he made the appropriate technical remarks in the course of the experiment, the instructor took a certain sadistic pleasure in repeating several times that, if he poured the solution too fast (*trop fort*), the whole thing could explode.

The patient experienced this as a sexual metaphor reactivating all the previously repressed sexual signifiers. What was taking place was, in effect, an actual unconscious sex act sustained throughout by distinctive signifiers: the red solution in the test tube; the test tube itself as a metaphor of the erect penis; the evaporating dish unconsciously fantasized as the female genital; the boiling up of the precipitate as a symbol of mounting orgasmic excitement; and last of all the signifier *trop fort* together with "the whole thing might explode," which repeated the explosion of orgastic abdominal spasms.

The gradual telescoping together of all these signifiers was manifested in an insidious heightening of anxiety as the experiment proceeded, as if it were a metaphor of the heightening of pleasure. Finally, the signifier *trop fort* triggered the involuntary urination, that is, the unconscious orgasm, and the ensuing loss of consciousness.

One last puzzling element remains to be specified in order to explain how the symptom took on its final shape. This element, the catalyst that brought about the unconscious metaphor of a sex act in the conscious form of self-mutilation, was a signifier that was to organize the chain of all the other signifying elements in the direction of this narcissistic bodily violence. Its discovery required additional investigative work to enable the patient's desire, held captive in the self-mutilation, to reveal its signification and thereby exorcise the symptom. The element in question had been set aside among the objects on the lab table where the experiment was being carried out. Near the evaporation dish a dissection kit was lying open, and among other instruments arranged in it were a scalpel and a razor.

This is striking evidence of the effect of repression and the metonymic displacement of the characteristic signifiers of the hysterical structure. While the patient was right in the middle of an unconscious love scene, a final signifier became the heir to the repressed erotic affect displaced onto a cutting instrument. Love and the accompanying sexual pleasure henceforth became incisive in the full sense of the word, since this key signifier polarized all the others into the formal symptom-picture of self-mutilation. From that time on, if one element of this signifying combination was suddenly brought into association with a signifier in reality, the ritual of the symptom was triggered.

The first occurrence of the symptom took the form of cutting of the breast. Because the breast was inscribed as one of the signifiers of sexual pleasure, cutting it with a razor blade was a metaphor for the act of coitus. The blood that flowed and streamed onto the patient's body represented the erotic connotations of the ski instructor's red outfit. The ritual of cutting was, furthermore, always preceded by a complete undressing that clearly evoked the signifiers marked out in the shower and pool episodes. That the cutting rituals invariably took place in a toilet or bathroom confirmed the ongoing importance of this signifier present in several of the patient's memories. Her isolation in these places also recalls the inscription of the screen signifier separating physical pleasure from the gaze or the presence of the other.

One detail of the symptomatic protocol bears the mark of the last signifiers comprising the unconscious chain. The cutting ritual was not complete until the blood had fully coagulated, just as the waning of the orgasm always brought about an irresistible wish to sleep after each such episode. We have here a consistent symptomatic restaging of the signifier of the loss of consciousness associated with the involuntary and uncontrollable urination.

It is not surprising to find a signifying sequence of the same order in the obsessional fantasy mentioned in the first interview. The man who showed up for an unforeseen visit is a generic counterpart of the man at the pool who addressed the patient unexpectedly from the other side of the cabana door. Just as she had not seen this man in reality, the man in the fantasy was anonymous and could never be described. The retreat into the bathroom also involved the recreation of a signifier common to several of the scenes described by the patient. In the fantasy she would go into the bathroom to fix her hair and makeup, which recalls her friend's lovemaking in a bathroom. In some respects the fantasy scenario expressed a similar intention: to make herself presentable for her unexpected male visitor. Moreover, in this reverie we can identify an unconscious signifying sequence that enacts, in reverse, certain situations in which the patient had found herself. What was the man behind the bathroom door doing with her friend? Making love? Quarreling? This questioning found its mirror-image counterpart in fantasy, when the patient would wonder what her visitor, on the other side of the door, imagined she herself was doing. Finally, this fantasy confirmed the potentially secretive nature of the pleasure experienced apart from the gaze or the presence of the other, in conformity with the scenes she recalled in the analysis.

*   *   *

On the basis of this clinical material we may conclude that a diagnosis is never—or at any rate not without some danger—based solely on the identification of a symptom. This case study, though fragmentary, illustrates the radical distinction between the symptom and structural traits.

A symptom is always the product of an overdetermined psychic elaboration, as Freud (1893–1895) was the first to observe in "Studies on Hysteria." The overdetermination of unconscious formations is, in turn, linked to the operation of the primary process. This clinical example shows the extent to which the mechanisms of metaphoric condensation and metonymic displacement of signifiers play an active role in the structuring of the symptom. In this sense, the symptom as such is always only a metaphor, that is, a signifying substitution, because its overdetermination is chiefly due to the fact that its manifest signifying substrate has replaced the latent signifier of desire and holds that desire captive (cf. Dor 1985).

Under these conditions the nature of the symptom assumes a signifying value that is random and unpredictable. The symptom is built up by successive signifying stratifications in which the selection of signifiers follows no fixed principle. In other words, the signifying ingredients constituting the symptom remain directly dependent on unconscious fantasies that operate selectively according to the combined action of metaphoric and metonymic processes.

On the other hand, in comparison with the relative indeterminacy of the choice of signifiers comprising the formations of the unconscious, we find an inescapable determinacy with regard to the management of the signifying material, which for the most part takes place outside of the subject's awareness. This management, characteristic of the structure's economy and profile, is specific to the way in which desire is handled. The mode of handling desire, and thus of bringing particular stable traits into play, is therefore what we need to determine in a diagnostic evaluation.

The problem of diagnosis, then, indirectly raises the question of the constancy of structural traits. If such constancy exists, it inevitably presupposes a certain stability in the organization of psychic structure. This will be the subject of the next chapter.

4

The Notion of Structure in Psychopathology

The notion of structure as it occurs in psychoanalysis, and more generally in the field of psychopathology, goes far beyond semiological and nosological considerations. And yet the misuse of the term "structure" in the world of contemporary thought sometimes makes it difficult to be precise in specifying its field of application.

From the formal point of view there is nothing better defined than a structure. Epistemologically, a structure is first and foremost an abstract model: a set of elements and the internal laws of composition applied to these elements. This formulation may not be entirely explicit in itself, but at least it has the advantage of defining, on the most general level, all the categories of structure, these being distinct from one another with respect to either the nature of the elements or the choice of laws pertaining to them.

The notion of structure as applied to a field of investigation is of essentially heuristic value. It is an operative tool that strategically favors discovery, because it brings to light apparently concealed relationships among the elements of a given domain. The structural model, in fact, is fruitful only above and beyond a certain mode of relation to objects, especially beyond the usual approach of descriptions, differentiations, and classifications of objects and their specific properties. The operative nature of the structural model always presupposes that approaches of this sort have been undertaken, but for the most part it requires that they be bracketed or even renounced. It is only on this condition that a structural conception can reveal the hidden relationships among objects and among their elements. Provided that there is a degree of coherence in the objects under consideration—that they come under the same heading or belong to the same grouping—such relationships can emerge. They have, from the outset, the status of laws demonstrating hitherto unnoticed properties. And these distinctive properties, in turn, determine a structure specific to the set of objects or elements to which the laws apply.

Let us look at the heuristic function of the structural approach in an example that is both classic and spectacular: the architectonic generalization of the geometric field.

Euclidian geometry is a structural system that, like any structure, includes elements and laws governing their reciprocal use within the system. What we are dealing with here, of course, is the set of basic geometric objects: the point, the straight line, the plane. The laws are of two kinds: axioms, that is, general properties accepted as true without having to be demonstrated (in Euclid's presentation, these axioms are called "postulates" or "principles"), and laws of internal composition (associative and distributive laws, etc.). All of Euclidian geometry thus opens out from these basic objects and these few laws.

The Fifth Postulate in this system (known as the Parallel Postulate) has always been considered problematic because it was not directly and simply evident like the other postulates and thus seemed more like a theorem than like a preliminary assumption. From the time of antiquity to the nineteenth century, mathematicians tried to find a way to get rid of it by showing that it could be deduced on the basis of demonstrative procedures.

. Without going into the details of this long speculative history, let us recall the names of some mathematical celebrities associated with these attempts at proof: Proclus and Ptolemy in the immediate post-Euclidian period, John Wallis in the seventeenth century, and Lambert, Legendre, and Gauss in the nineteenth. But the three most important names to keep in mind are those of mathematicians who found an original solution to this problem at about the same time: Lobachevsky in 1826, Bolyaï in 1831, and Riemann in 1854.

All three took up the hypothesis of Sacchéri's demonstration, one whose basis was sound although Sacchéri made several unfortunate errors in reasoning. This is an attempt to establish the truth of the Fifth Postulate by proving that it is the result of its own negation. In this case, then, what has to be shown is that falsity implies truth, a fairly common mathematical procedure. The first stage of this demonstration involves the rectangle ABCD:

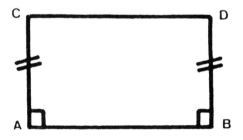

The two opposite sides AC and BD are presumed to be equal and perpendicular to AB. The demonstration involves maintaining that, if the Fifth Postulate is true, C and D must be right angles. The truth of the Fifth Postulate consists in eliminating the twofold possibility that these angles are either greater or less than 90°, either obtuse or acute.

Sacchéri tried to make use of these two possibilities by introducing them one by one into the Euclidean system. In each case, it was only errors in reasoning that enabled him to claim the absurdity of the new geometrical systems that he had constructed on the basis of these two original suppositions; he never managed to demonstrate it. Bolyaï established the same type of geometry. Riemann, however, succeeded in explaining without contradiction the hypothesis of the obtuse angle, constructing an elliptical geometry in which no parallel line can be drawn through a point outside a straight line.

These non-Euclidean geometries were of great importance in modern mathematics, but of more general epistemological interest is their rigorous notion of structure. Since, in Riemannian geometry, we cannot draw a parallel to a straight line, we have to accept the idea of a positively curved space such that angles A, B, and C add up to more than 180°:

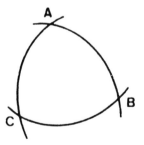

The less pronounced the curvature, the closer we come to Euclidean space. Thus, when the radius of curvature is infinite, we are back with Euclidean geometry; inversely, Lobachevskian geometry is a negative system in which angles A, B, and C add up to less than 180°:

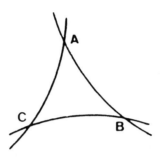

Here again we can follow the same reasoning with regard to Euclid's geometry, which thus appears as a special case of non-Euclidean systems, a special case in which angles A, B, and C add up to 180°:

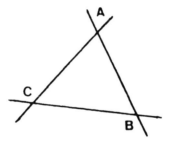

In this sense, Riemann's geometry, like Lobachevsky's, is a more general structure than Euclid's, which, consequently, is a limiting structure in the field of non-Euclidean geometries, a substructure. Euclidean space is just one possible space among all intelligible and consistent geometric spaces. With the structure of metageometries, we move to a higher level of intelligibility: though Euclid's geometry is a coherent structure, Riemann's is one that includes it. Thus a more general structure was elaborated, one that could account for a greater amount of information. This hierarchy in the generalization of structures is the most obvious proof of the fundamentally heuristic nature of the procedure.

With regard to psychopathology, even if we never match the rigor of formal speculation, the use of the concept of structure is equally fruitful. It enables us to go beyond the semiological and nosographic approach by locating the investigation, right from the beginning, outside the realm of purely qualitative or differential considerations. Freud was well aware of this when, introducing the principle of psychic causality into the field of psychopathology, he implicitly promoted a structural approach.

Such an approach makes for greater intelligibility. (We might almost speak of Bachelard's notion of epistemological rupture here.) By way of illustration, let us compare with Freud's work that of a psychopathologist like Havelock Ellis. The difference is significant. Ellis (1905–1942) gathers together an enormous amount of information about sexual psychopathology in a work that is a rich and exhaustive description of many clinical categories. But it is soon evident that his clinical interest in understanding psychopathological processes is hardly greater than that of a restaurant guide when it comes to the art of cooking.

In contrast, when we look at any part of Freud's work, we are continually being introduced to another approach to psychopathology. We are no longer dealing with a catalogue of semiological data but with structural dynamics, if only because the argument is always developed in a direct or indirect relation to metapsychology. This metapsychology is not a mere collection of theoretical speculations. It is constantly rooted in three fundamental dimensions: the topographic, dynamic, and economic perspectives. These three registers precisely define the substrate that characterizes as structural the entirety of Freud's investigations.

We must look at one more thing if we are to hold that the notion of structure is always applicable to its object. This connection is not always explicit in Freud, but his successors have fully examined and clarified the adequacy of this theory. At the present time, then, we are able to develop a model of fundamental psychic structuration in which internal regulation gives rise to various structural profiles whose stability can be ascertained on the basis of certain specific traits.

5

Psychic Structures and the Phallic Function

For every subject, the structuring of a psychic organization takes place in the context of oedipal attachments, that is, in the agitated unfolding of the relation to the phallic function. Although this relation promotes order insofar as it brings about organization, it also—and for this very reason—promotes disorder, since psychic structuration has the essential feature of being irreversibly determined. How are we to understand that order can lead to disorder? This basic paradox reveals how structuration can be a decisive step in psychic economy and how, at the very same time, this economy can be the primary agent of psychopathology.

To explain how this can be so, we can make use of an analogy that, although it is metaphoric, illustrates the paradoxical workings of the psychic economy. This argument is drawn from present-day molecular biology and involves the self-preservation of biological structures. Without going into specific biochemical details, we will make use of the underlying principle (cf. Lwoff 1970).

An organism can be considered to be a complex machine, in that it involves increasing thresholds of complexity. Like any structured machine, it must be supplied with energy. But we cannot take the analogy between organism and machine any further, since organisms have a fundamental property that they do not share with even the most complex machines. The structure of a machine remains self-identical when the machine is at rest. The equation illustrating the state of the organism at rest is as follows:

organism + energy supply $\rightarrow$ organism + waste products + heat

This equation means that an organism cannot remain structured as such when it is supplied with energy. Even if it produces no work, the organism always requires a certain amount of energic capital to persist in its structures.

Several conclusions follow from this observation. First, biological order, if it is to be maintained, requires energy that must be degraded. Second, in the absence of degradable energy, the organism is subject to a biological law of increasing disorder, in the course of which every ordered structure is disorganized step by step, up to the point of maximal disorder that is death.

This increase in disorder is referred to as biological entropy. Generally speaking, the law of entropy is expressed in physics by the Second Law of Thermodynamics, or the Carnot-Clausius Principle. No living or inert phenomenon escapes this principle, since none escapes the degradation of energy, which is irreversible. The entropic change that occurs in this irreversible movement is measured by an increasing probability of disorder. The measure of disorder constituting entropy is given in the formula:

entropy = K log. D, where K represents the Boltzmann constant and D the measure of disorder.

Since entropy is a measure of disorder, it is easy to obtain a measure of order by the inverse formula of negative entropy:

$$N = K \log. \frac{1}{D}$$

In accordance with the Carnot-Clausius Principle, every organism deprived of energy tends toward increasing entropy, that is, increasing disorder. Conversely, an organism that maintains order in its structures permanently decreases its entropy. Metaphorically, we can say that it is supplied with negative entropy.

Thus the organism, in its functioning, is the site of a certain paradoxical economy. On the one hand, nothing could be clearer than that it undergoes an irreversible degradation that leads it toward death. On the other hand, nothing could be clearer than that such an organism contains and reproduces a negative entropy of structure that perpetuates an economy of order in this irreversible disorder. In other words, if the increase in entropy is to last as long as possible until it reaches its maximal state, the organism must continually deduct negative entropy. This is the paradoxical economy of the functioning of biological structure.

Even with the limitations of a metaphorical analogy, we can find a similar paradoxical economy in the case of psychic structures. As is the case with biological structures, psychic functioning tends toward the probability of maximal disorder, that is, an irreversible increase in entropy if the psychic apparatus is not permanently supplied with negative entropy. This constant relation to negative entropy, therefore, maintains psychic structure in a kind of order that assures its stability.

If we pursue the analogy, we can think of the increase in psychic entropy as a process directly proportional to the increase in *jouissance*. *Jouissance* is thus the most likely measure of psychic disorder. (This presupposes, of course, that we take into account Lacan's radical distinction between *jouissance* and pleasure.) As for disorder, it is all the more irreversible because it is subject to the constant force of desire.

As with biological structures, if the psychic apparatus cannot "consume" energy, the psychic organization is degraded until it reaches the point of maximal disorder manifested as a certain state of "psychic death."

How does the psychic apparatus sustain a relation to negative entropy so as to preserve its structure? We first have to understand what this metaphoric term *negative entropy* means in the case of the psychic apparatus. If *jouissance* is the index of the ongoing increase in disorder, this implies that castration is what introduces a measure of order in the economy of psychic structure. In this sense, negative entropy is assessed with reference to castration. As a result, structural order is instituted by the phallic order.

Psychic structure has to "degrade" or "metabolize" energy so as to maintain its order. The only degradable order in this metaphoric analogy is that of the desire of the other. The negative entropy of the psyche can therefore be understood as the degradation of the energy of the other's desire. However, this metabolism of the energy of the other's desire leads to order only to the extent that it is governed by a certain kind of symbolic relation to the phallus. Without this symbolic mediation of the phallic function, the relation to the desire of the other tends to be constituted blindly, in a mode of entropic *jouissance*. Under these conditions, the relation of the subject's desire to the desire of the other follows the irreversible course of a pure increase in disorder.

What justifies us in sustaining the analogy between the irreducibility of biological entropy and of psychic entropy? Indeed, this analogy holds up only if we can discern in psychic structures the same type of paradoxical economy we encountered in biological structures. This type of economy requires us to accept the necessity of maintaining more and more order, so that the increase in disorder will not occur too quickly but, on the contrary, will last as long as possible.

In the case of psychic structure, this amounts to recognizing that the subject's desire must continually submit to the phallic function so as to minimize the irreversibility of *jouissance*. Is it really true that *jouissance* increases entropically? Psychopathology certainly keeps on confirming this increase in disorder. In fact, the unfolding of entropy is in the very nature of desire.

With regard to his desire, the subject initially tends to set himself up as the sole and unique object of the other's desire. *Jouissance* is proportionate to this dynamic of desire and must expand lethally if nothing sets a limit to it—that is, if the subject's desire is not inscribed in the dimension of lack. The phallic function is exactly what promotes this inscription. Indeed, the subject's desire finds the symbolic mediation that inscribes it in lack only through the relation it maintains with the phallus.

This being the case, we can uphold the analogy as long as we think of lack as psychic negative entropy. Psychic structure is maintained in a certain order if the subject's desire is sustained by the desire of the other when it encounters lack there. Conversely, because structure is organized by a prior lack, desire is continually reborn as self-identical, as an aspiration to repeat the *jouissance* that is trying to fill the lack. Psychic structure, then, complies with a paradoxical economy in which its own stability resides.

But it is one thing to describe at its most fundamental level the unique nature of the economy that governs psychic structures, another to understand how this economy of desire, operating in accordance with the phallic function, can bring about different types of structures. The memory of oedipal attachments takes on its meaning in the context of this distinction, since it is in the vicissitudes of these attachments that the subject negotiates his relation to the phallus and hence to the synergy of desire and lack.

Without going into the details of the oedipal saga (see Dor 1985, Ch. 12), let us just recall that this dynamic unfolds in the dialectic of being and having—in other words, in a movement of psychic elaboration that leads the subject from a position where he is identified with the mother's phallus to one where, renouncing that identification and accepting symbolic castration, he tends to identify either with the one who is presumed to have the phallus, or, alternatively, with the one who is presumed not to have it. This decisive operation takes place as an inaugural process of symbolization that Lacan calls the metaphor of the Name-of-the-Father.

It is important to emphasize certain stages in this oedipal dialectic, stages that are crucial for the subject when the stakes of desire mobilized in relation to the phallus are especially favorable to the formation of particular structural organizations. This is the case with the perverse structure (as with the others: obsessional, hysteric, and psychotic), whose organization can be defined on the basis of characteristic precipitating elements. These elements intervene on the terrain of a fundamental psychic structuration, and it is here, in the triangulation of the mutual desires of the mother, the father, and the child, that we can perceive their internal relations. But whatever the nature of these precipitating elements that irreversibly determine structure, all of them remain fundamentally subject to the signifier that ballasts them.

In this sense, we can say that there is no morality in psychoanalysis, because structure does not change. This is no oracular pronouncement, nor is it a totalitarian or ecumenical declaration of principle. At most, what it does is remind us that, as psychically structured subjects, we are simply effects of the signifier. Though structure works under the direction of these effects, we are never its masters. We may cling in imagination to the idea that we have some input into this mastery if we place our fantasy under the banner of some system of values. But whatever the choice of such a system—religious, social, political, familial, educational— we can change nothing. Similarly, we always have some say in the choice of one or another direction favorable to virtue, but this will not change the fact that, in saying this word, we are always denying it in the very act of articulating it.

The Freudian adage that the ego is not master in its own house achieves canonical status only in terms of what follows from it. And it is these implications that enable us to identify a field and a locus of discourse that are properly psychoanalytic. Though no one is obliged to subscribe to it, it remains the case that the Freudian discovery revealed a truth that corresponds precisely to the structure of the one who announces it. Though it is always only "half said," as Lacan notes, it is all the more insistent because it recalls the order of structure and desire that tries to make its way through it. As Charles Melman (1984) puts it, "What is there to be angry about, to struggle with? Lacan calls Other the linguistic system that governs our alienations, those alienations that need no legislator; but if its power is solely a function of its place, can we fight against a place?" (p. 10). The indisputable dimension of the symbolic, then, ultimately remains decisive in the choice of psychic structure.

The whole of Freud's work, as Lacan tried so hard to remind us in explaining it, invites us to take the full measure of this primary function of the symbolic in the course of psychic destiny. Before we look more deeply into the perverse structure, we must therefore return to the Freudian theories that establish the most fundamental metapsychological and clinical features of this mode of psychic economy.

Part II

The Structural Logic of the Perverse Process

6

The Classical Conception of the Perversions

We have to be very careful in approaching the world of the perversions, because it is still true that this category has come to include considerations that are often alien to the field of psychopathology proper.

It would be wrong to think that the psychoanalytic meaning has conclusively subverted classical etiological notions of the perverse process. Some of these notions persist stubbornly, undermining Freud's theorization. In the best cases, when this theorization is included in the understanding of the perverse process, it is often shorn of its most original implications, integrated into a series of concepts of psychopathology that neutralize its impact. Evidence for this can be found in current writings that persist in offering completely eclectic etiological theories and inconsistent clinical findings.

For example, consider the weak theoretical and clinical hodgepodge of Charles Porot's (1975) articles on the perversions (cf. Bardenat 1975). Spending some time looking at these arguments enables us to appreciate the extraordinarily fruitful contribution of psychoanalysis to the understanding of the structural locus in which the perverse process is organized and deployed.

First of all, we find the distinction, as standard as it is pointless, between perversion and perversity. Perversity is said to involve a kind of malice at work in certain acts of an individual, and we are thus called upon to make moral judgments on behavior. It therefore becomes difficult to go on to distinguish perversity from perversion, since we are given only a single term, *pervert*, as the author sensibly notes, to differentiate between the two (p. 497). What, then, are we to understand by *perversity*? According to Henri Ey (in Porot, p. 497), we are dealing with an immoral choice in the normative rules of behavior; the pervert not only abandons himself to evil but desires it. This maladjustment with regard to behavioral norms is said to be the result of immaturity, of developmental arrest at a stage whose structure of affectivity becomes the law of the individual's existence.

This claim is highly ambiguous. As soon as we raise the issue of fixation at a stage of psychic evolution capable of establishing a permanent structure of affective functioning, we are moving into a different field, away from normative evaluation and toward a metapsychological argument concerning the structure of the perversions. This being so, there seems to be no reason to distinguish a disposition such as perversity.

However (to follow Porot's argument), it is as though, in contrast to the perversions, perversity is supposed to arise from an episodic and limited behavioral orientation, one that can even be discerned in so called "normal" people. For example, this is said to be true of certain acts of physical and/or moral cruelty committed under the sway of passion (jealousy, hatred, mystical or politi cal exaltation); on a more banal level are various acts of vandalism. Such acts of perversity, we are told, may be hidden behind a tendency to subversion, provocation, scandal, and the like. In general, perversity as defined here remains exclusively bound up with social or medico-legal criteria.

In one of his *Etudes Psychiatriques*, Henri Ey (1950, pp. 238–246) goes still further by focusing the problem of perversity directly on the notion of freedom, raising the thorny issue of whether or not there is deliberate intentionality in the perverse act with regard to the premeditation of harm, an intentionality that would represent a voluntary liberation of the bad tendencies of nature. We find a similar assessment in a more "technical" guise when the discussion turns to whether or not the perverse act is preceded by a pathological deterioration of the personality. Nevertheless, once the factor of psychopathology is introduced, we subtly leave the field of perversity for that of perversion proper. For a distinction of this kind tends to circumscribe the domain of the perversions to a set of permanent pathological aptitudes, that is, to what is usually called a deviation from normal tendencies. We are referred to that part of the unconscious known as instinct; hence Ey's generic definition of "instinctual perversions."

But as soon as perversions are associated with deviant instinctual processes, we face the highly complex problem of defining their nature. Ey (p. 498) points out that greed, for example, is derived from the instinct for self-preservation but is related on the social level to altruism. Procuring is a perversion of the instinct for affiliation, but it makes use of sexual depravity. Instinctual compromises result in laziness that appears as a perversion on the level of collective life, while on the level of self-preservation it corresponds to the biological law of economy of effort. Nor can perversions be classified according to their consequences. The vain person and the spendthrift do no major harm to others or to themselves. On the other hand, Ey notes, every harmful act may be directly dependent on a perversion on the agent's part.

This type of analysis shows how hard it is to define the problematics of the perversions with any rigor. If we are to remove the perversions from this welter of pseudo-ethical considerations, we must take a different tack, leaving the domain of the phenomenological consideration of "the personality of the pervert." Such consideration will get us nowhere when it comes to understanding the perverse process.

Even if we agree with Ey (p. 498) that the organic substrate of instinctual perversion cannot be revealed by current methods of physiological investigation, he does seem to believe in this possibility on the basis both of causal factors having to do with heredity and of experimental evidence for "acquired perversions." He supports his argument with observations of the effects of encephalitis, encephalopathy, accidental intoxication, and even chronic intoxication of the so-called "luxury" type, such as alcoholism. Moreover, Ey claims, as psychic abnormalities the perversions are usually combined with intellectual deficits such as retardation or with constitutional imbalances such as hyperemotivity and instability. Similarly, it is argued, the perversions may be expressed as a result of intercurrent psychoses.

The social behavior of the pervert is said to depend on his intellectual level; his degree of social adaptation varies as a function of his character. A number of other pathological factors can intervene in the direction of the perversions. Thus the epilepsies can dangerously aggravate perverse reactions, and hysteria can act as a catalyst for them by virtue of the instinctual abnormality and the crises that are characteristic of it. Furthermore, the perverse process is said to become apparent very soon in the development of the personality, given prodromal signs such as malice, cruelty, violence, indiscipline, deviousness, and lying, faults that the family and the educational system are unable to restrain.

On the basis of such observational data concerning the abnormal personality, Ey (p. 499) constructs a typical profile of the pervert as someone whose behavior is governed by his desires and appetites without regard for others, or by the lack of habitual moderating factors. The pervert is inclined toward substance abuse and gambling, along with cheating, vagrancy, desertion, theft and its multiple variants, destructiveness, arson, prostitution, and so forth. He tends to associate with criminals, which extends his field of action and renders him more dangerous. He has no moral sense as such.

Thus, by a secret slippage, perversion is assimilated to delinquency. It is to be treated similarly, by the creation of special facilities under appropriate medical and legal regulation. There could be no better evidence for the poverty of this line of argumentation, one that is parasitical on the field of psychopathology, which, if it can be said to exist at all, is ratified only by moral and ideological norms that entirely preempt any clinical understanding.

There is, however, an aspect of the perversions that we have not discussed yet: the sexual perversions, subtly dissociated from the "instinctual perversions." It is true that, historically, they have been considered separately and, for certain authors, seem to remain apart. How are they defined? According to Ey (p. 500), they involve the quest for sexual gratification outside of physical coupling with a subject of the same species and the opposite sex. A good example of this point of view, still current, was given by the French alienist Ball (1888) in the nineteenth century.

According to this definition, sexual perversions are divided into two kinds: perversions with regard to their object (homosexuality, pedophilia, necrophilia, and bestiality) and perversions with regard to their means (fetishism, sadism, masochism). A final class of perverts is made up of subjects who derive full sexual gratification from acts belonging to foreplay, an absurd assortment of voyeurs, exhibitionists, and those who enjoy brushing up against others.

Despite the occasional survival of organicist etiologies for sexual perversions, most writers seem to agree that they are of psychological origin. Nevertheless, this hypothesis is still accompanied by rather ambiguous views. For, in fact, these causal explanations that borrow from psychoanalysis almost always fail to draw the logical implications of unconscious processes. Typical of these compromises is Ey's account (1950, p. 500). Here psychoanalysis is acknowledged for having pointed out the ongoing yet unconscious influence of polymorphous infantile sexuality, and yet the author goes on to contradict this causal explanation by adducing ideological issues, claiming that perversion may sometimes occur without an inner struggle; the sick pervert who experiences his illness as a painful obsession is to be distinguished from the one who is simply vicious.

Although this concept of the perversions remains current, it is a good illustration of the semiological incoherence and clinical inconsistency that mark the approach to the perverse process and impede its understanding. Beyond the purely differential and comparative approach in which distinctions are made according to ideological criteria, this analysis of the perversions involves a thoroughgoing confusion between perverse traits and perverse manifestations. Such ambiguities make the perverse process seem to be a relatively atypical disposition without structural specificity. Combining behavioral observations and normative judgments leaves no room for an investigation of the psychogenic etiology of the perversions. In particular, we find no description of a set of metapsychological processes representing, to say the least, the remarkable singularity of a type of psychic functioning. Although psychic causality is presupposed in order to account for the onset of perversion, it is implicitly denied, at the same time, by the lack of appropriate reference points. Without rigorous etiological criteria, the perversions can be understood only in terms of universal norms. This clinical weakness ultimately shows the failure to recognize the only locus of intelligibility in which the perversions can be defined: the psychosexual field.

In *The Language of Psycho-Analysis*, Laplanche and Pontalis (1973, pp. 306–309) are careful to note that we cannot speak of the perversions except in relation to sexuality. Even if Freud distinguishes several drives, it is always in the context of the sexual drives that he describes the dynamics of the perverse process. If behaviors other than sexual behaviors appear "deviant" in a subject, the recourse to perversion is not automatically called for, especially since clinical psychoanalysis can demonstrate frequent correlations between such deviant behaviors and sexuality. In this sense, the psychoanalytic concept of the perversions is more economical and more rigorous in its operative and instrumental nature. Its approach to the perversions is illuminated both on the level of clinical intelligibility and the level of therapeutic effectiveness.

The psychoanalytic theory of the perversions is based on a largely metapsychological set of concepts. Even if metapsychology often needs to be put in question with regard to its implications, it nevertheless opens the possibility for genuine clinical and theoretical reflection. In contrast, the intrusion of ideology preempts this possibility of interpellation; every therapeutic opening is hidden to the extent that the field of intelligibility is itself interfered with, overdetermined, by the predominance of norms tacitly containing a prohibition.

Clinical psychoanalysis, however, does not always escape this type of interference. One of the prime examples of this overdetermination is the issue of homosexuality. How is this problematic framed in clinical psychoanalysis? How do we define the goal of treatment?

Though the question may seem trivial, it is constantly raised in everyday practice. What happens when certain analysts make the disappearance of the patient's homosexuality the primary aim of treatment? Only an ideological argument implicitly based on sexual norms can underlie such a practice. But with the intrusion of norms we leave the strictly analytic register. The only norms that exist in clinical psychoanalysis are those that govern the space of the treatment. At the very most, what we are dealing with are the so-called fundamental rules that engage analyst and patient alike in a contract necessary to the development of the analytic work. Although these few rules of treatment are required as a matter of principle, all other norms are forbidden.

This being the case, heterosexuality is a possible outcome of the treatment of a homosexual patient. But it can in no way be defined as a necessary outcome, since this would presuppose the undermining of the analysis by normative considerations that are irreconcilable with the unpredictable nature of the unconscious.

This brief example shows how useless it is to hand over the problematics of the perversions to the realm of norms. But it also reminds us how rigorous we must be in our clinical approach to these conditions whose psychopathological manifestations involve issues of normativity as well as normality. This is why our vigilance must first of all be tested out on the level of a metapsychological foundation that can explain the basic structure of the perversions.

7

The Notion of Drive in the Perverse Process

The drive, central in Freudian metapsychology, is a pivotal element of the psychic economy of the perversions, because the drive is crucial in the evolution of infantile sexuality and is also the psychic vector that actualizes the perverse process.

The concept of the drive appears explicitly in Freud's *Three Essays on the Theory of Sexuality* (1905b): "The fact of the existence of sexual needs in human beings and animals is expressed in biology by the assumption of a 'sexual instinct,' on the analogy of the instinct of nutrition, that is, of hunger" (p. 135). With this introduction of the concept of the drive Freud begins his first essay, "The Sexual Aberrations," which covers the psychopathology of the perversions as it was defined in the classical tradition. The notion of drive enables Freud to specify a twofold definition of a "sexual aberration" as either a deviation relative to the object of the sexual drive or a deviation relative to its aim. The structure of the essay is highly informative:

1. Deviations in Respect of the Sexual Object
   A. Inversion
   B. Sexually immature persons and animals as objects
2. Deviations in Respect of the Sexual Aim
   A. Anatomical extensions
   B. Fixations of preliminary sexual aims
3. The Perversions in General
4. The Sexual Instinct in Neurotics
5. Component Instincts and Erotogenic Zones
6. Reasons for the Apparent Preponderance of Perverse Sexuality in the Psychoneuroses
7. Intimation of the Infantile Character of Sexuality

This outline in itself is indicative of the way in which Freud is trying to approach the perversions. Three general observations may be made here.

First, with the heading "Sexual Aberrations," Freud is adopting an entirely classical nomenclature, one that we find, for example, in Krafft-Ebing's (1869) division of the perversions into two groups, one in which the aim of the action is perverse (sadism, masochism, fetishism, and exhibitionism) and a group in which the object is perverse (homosexuality, pedophilia, gerontophilia, zoophilia, and autoerotism). Yet, beyond this reference to the classical theorists, Freud's originality lies in his linking sexual aberration to the concept of drive from the outset.

Second, the concept of perversion is not introduced right away in Freud's classification. While the traditional contrast between inversion and perversion seems to correspond to the contrast between deviation with regard to object and deviation with regard to aim, Freud does not explicitly use the term *perversion* until the section on deviations relating to the sexual aim:

The normal sexual aim is regarded as being the union of the genitals in the act known as copulation, which leads to a release of the sexual tension and a temporary extinction of the sexual instinct. . . . *But even in the most normal sexual process we may detect rudiments which, if they had developed, would have led to the deviations described as 'perversions.'* . . . Perversions are sexual activities which either (a) extend, in an anatomical sense, beyond the regions of the body that are designed for sexual union, or (b) linger over the intermediate relations to the sexual object which should normally be traversed rapidly on the path toward the final sexual aim. [pp. 149–150, emphasis added]

Thus Freud sees perversion not only as a deviation of the aim of the drive but also as an exaggeration of the normal sexual process. If, in so doing, he seems to break with the classical division of the perversions (deviation regarding aim *and* deviation regarding object), this is because he anticipates the very particular status of the object of the sexual drives, an object that he will later say has no necessary specificity. Moreover, in stating the kinship between the perverse sexual process and the normal one, Freud clearly distances himself from all the classical theories in which the perversion are understood as deviations from the norm. For Freud, perversion is inscribed within the norm right from the beginning:

It is natural that medical men, who first studied perversions in outstanding examples and under special conditions, should have been inclined to regard them, like inversion, as indications of degeneracy or disease. Nevertheless, it is even easier to dispose of that view in this case than in that of inversion. Everyday experience has shown that most of these extensions, or at any rate the less severe of them, are constituents which are rarely absent from the sexual life of healthy people, and are judged by them no differently from other intimate events. If circumstances favour such an occurrence, normal people too can substitute a perversion of this kind for the normal sexual aim for quite a time, or can find place for the one alongside the other. No healthy person, it appears, can fail to make some addition that might be called perverse to the normal sexual aim. . . . [p. 160]

A third and final observation can be made about this first essay on the sexual aberrations. Starting with the section entitled "The Perversions in General," the text turns toward generalizations about sexuality. Is it really a coincidence that this broadened focus occurs precisely in the context of the perversions?

Perversion emphasizes a certain plasticity of the sexual drive. And, as Freud notes, this modification in the aim of the instinctual process plays a more or less legitimate role in normal sexual life. Thus the sexual process as a whole is located within these instinctual fluctuations. Freud develops his argument gradually. He first analyzes these fluctuations in "people who at least approximate to the normal" (p. 163) and then goes on to establish a direct connection between neurosis and perversion:

[Psychoanalysis] shows that it is by no means only at the cost of the so-called *normal* sexual instinct that these symptoms originate—at any rate such is not exclusively or mainly the case; they also give expression (by conversion) to instincts which would be described as *perverse* in the widest sense of the word if they could be expressed directly in phantasy and action without being diverted from consciousness. Thus symptoms are formed in part at the cost of *abnormal* sexuality; *neuroses are, so to say, the negative of perversions.*

The sexual instinct of psychoneurotics exhibits all the aberrations which we have studied as variations of normal, and as manifestations of abnormal, sexual life. [pp. 165–166, emphasis in original]

With this generalization Freud confirms a statement he had previously made regarding the drive process at work in the perversions, namely the complex nature of the sexual instinct: "[W]e have found that some of the perversions which we have examined are only made intelligible if we assume the convergence of several motive forces. . . . This gives us a hint that perhaps the sexual instinct itself may be no simple thing, but put together from components which have come apart again in the perversions" (p. 162).

Thus the study of the perversions leads Freud to the notion of the component instinct, which he explores in detail following the comparison of neurosis and perversion. And so it is not surprising, but quite logical, to find that the two final sections of the essay shift the focus to the perverse process in neurotics and, more generally, to the very basis of infantile sexuality. In neurotics, as in the child, the component instincts set in motion the entire sexual dynamic. It is because perverse sexuality is subject to the component instincts that the famous polymorphous perversity lies at the heart of infantile sexual organization.

Freud thus theorizes that these instinctual components of sexuality, at first autonomous, come together at a second stage, the time of puberty, around the primacy of the genital zone. Because of the way its partial components function, infantile sexuality is necessarily perverse, the play of "fragmented sexual activities" (Laplanche and Pontalis 1973, p. 75) imposing objects and aims other than the normal ones. These partial instincts, however, may persist as perverse tendencies during foreplay in the normal sex act. The organization of perversions in the adult thus finds its legitimate explanation in the reappearance of one or more components of infantile sexuality. In other words, the perversions represent a regression to a prior stage of libidinal development.

In Freud's view, then, perverse sexuality is less a marginal phenomenon of the sexual process than it is the very basis of normal sexuality, an inevitable disposition in the psychosexual evolution of every subject. Perversion ceases to be the object of ideological judgments, since it is no longer considered to be a deviation or an aberration of the sexual process.

In later works, Freud offers additional metapsychological refinements to this initial approach to the perversions. In "Instincts and Their Vicissitudes" (1915), he rigorously defines the aim and the object of the drive. These new observations allow for a better understanding of perverse sexuality, especially with regard to the plasticity of modes of instinctual satisfaction:

> The aim [Ziel] of an instinct is in every instance satisfaction, which can only be obtained by removing the state of stimulation at the source of the instinct. But although the ultimate aim of each instinct remains unchangeable, there may yet be different paths leading to the same ultimate aim; so that an instinct may be found to have various nearer or intermediate aims, which are combined or interchanged with one another. Experience permits us also to speak of instincts which are "inhibited in their aim," in the case of processes which are allowed to make some advance toward instinctual satisfaction but are then inhibited or deflected. We may suppose that even processes of this kind involve a partial satisfaction. [p. 122]

Freud introduces another fundamental clarification in connection with the object of the sexual drive. Such an object is totally variable and hence is chosen as a possible object of satisfaction only as a function of the subject's history:

> The object [Objekt] of an instinct is the thing in regard to which or through which the instinct is able to achieve its aim. It is what is most variable about an instinct and is not originally connected with it, but becomes assigned to it only in consequence of being peculiarly fitted to make satisfaction possible.

The object is not necessarily something extraneous: it may equally well be a part of the subject's own body. It may be changed any number of times in the course of the vicissitudes which the instinct undergoes during its existence; and highly important parts are played by this displacement of instinct. It may happen that the same object serves for the satisfaction of several instincts simultaneously. . . . A particularly close attachment of the instinct to its object is distinguished by the term "fixation." This frequently occurs at very early periods of the development of an instinct and puts an end to its mobility through its intense opposition to detachment. [pp. 122–123]

Indeed, just as the study of the perversions contradicts the idea of a predetermined sexual aim and object associated with genitality, the study of infantile sexuality proves the absence of such specificity in favor of a multiplicity of objects and aims. Freud makes immediate use of these conclusions about the mobility of instinctual aims and objects in sexuality:

This much can be said by way of a general characterization of the sexual instincts. They are numerous, emanate from a great variety of organic sources, act in the first instance independently of one another, and only achieve a more or less complete synthesis at a late stage. The aim which each of them strives for is the attainment of "organ-pleasure"; only when synthesis is achieved do they enter the service of the reproductive function and thereupon become generally recognizable as sexual instincts. At their first appearance they are attached to the instincts of self-preservation, from which they only gradually become separated; in their choice of object, too, they follow the paths that are indicated to them by the ego-instincts. A portion of them remains associated with the ego-instincts throughout life and furnishes them with libidinal components, which in normal functioning easily escape notice and are revealed clearly only by the onset of illness. They are distinguished by possessing the capacity to act vicariously for one another to a wide extent and by being able to change their objects readily. [pp. 125–126]

Freud singles out four types of instinctual vicissitude: repression and sublimation on the one hand, reversal into the opposite and turning against the self on the other, the latter two being directly involved in the perversions.

This metapsychological supplement enables Freud to solve a problem that had remained pending in the *Three Essays*. With regard to sexual aberrations, he had distinguished between deviations relating to object and those relating to aim. In concrete terms, this corresponded to the difference between inversions and perversions.

The concepts of reversal into the opposite and turning against the self of the instinctual process radically blur this distinction. Freud calls attention to two different mechanisms in reversal into the opposite. The instinct may turn around from activity to passivity, or the very content of the instinctual process may be reversed. The examples Freud adduces to illustrate the first type are taken from the domain of the perversions: sadism / masochism and voyeurism / exhibitionism. In both cases, the reversal involves only the aims of the instinct: "The active aim (to torture, to look at) is replaced by the passive aim (to be tortured, to be looked at)" (p. 127). As for reversal of content, it is best illustrated by the transformation of love into hate.

With regard to turning against the self, Freud once again finds examples in the perversions, except that now the point of the process is the change of object, while the aim remains the same: "The turning round of an instinct upon the subject's own self is made plausible by the reflection that masochism is actually sadism turned round upon the subject's own ego, and that exhibitionism includes looking at his own body. Analytic observation, indeed, leaves us in no doubt that the masochist shares in the enjoyment of the assault upon himself, and that the exhibitionist shares in the enjoyment of [the sight of] his exposure" (p. 127).

This elaboration of the concept of the drive clarifies a number of fundamental points. The perversions are now shown to be an inherent part of psychosexual developmental processes. The whole series of ideological and normativizing notions associated with the perversions is rendered null and void. Yet despite this major advance in the understanding of the perverse process, we are still far from a structural approach to the perversions. Were it not for the interaction between the perversions and the neuroses noted by Freud ("neuroses are, so to say, the negative of perversions" [1905b, p. 165]), we would have no reason to posit the autonomy of a perverse structure. At this stage of Freud's theorizing, the perversions are specified only insofar as they are the counterpart of the neuroses. This connection suggests that, in reality, the perversions actualize modes of sexual satisfaction that are quite similar to those at work in all the neuroses.

In the neuroses, the perverse components of sexuality have no concrete outcome. Rejected as immediately possible actualizations, they nevertheless remain present in disguised forms. Thus Freud observes that "symptoms are formed in part at the cost of abnormal sexuality" (p. 165). A misunderstanding has arisen here, to the effect that, in contrast to the neurotic, the pervert does not make use of repression: he enacts directly, in reality, what the neurotic represses in favor of the substitute formation of morbid symptoms. Such explanations do not stand up to a thorough metapsychological examination.

The initial decipherment of the perverse process in terms of drives soon proved inadequate. Freud was to return to the problematics of the perversions several times in the course of his later work. Other major metapsychological concepts such as the disavowal of reality, the disavowal of castration, and the splitting of the ego would come to play a primary role in the explanation of the perverse process. These new theoretical and clinical investigations, based on the analysis of fetishism, are all the more important because they closely overlap with the pathology of the psychoses. As we shall see, they therefore enable us to observe not only the structural proximity of the perversions and the psychoses but also the uniqueness of transsexual pathology.

8

Disavowal of Reality, Disavowal of Castration, and Splitting of the Ego

Freud did not develop the concept of disavowal in the context of the perversions as such. This defense mechanism is first mentioned in 1923, and Freud refers to it constantly throughout his later work.

He initially mentions disavowal in direct connection with castration, as is clearly suggested in the 1923 paper "The Infantile Genital Organization." Observing little girls, the boy notices that not everyone has a penis. He denies this lack, convincing himself that the girl's penis is small and will grow bigger or was once there and was taken away. The lack of a penis is believed to be the result of castration, and the child must now consider castration with regard to his own body. Disavowal is presented as a defensive process in the face of castration. And the contradiction that Freud notes between observation and preconception anticipates the formal appearance of the concept of disavowal in "Some Psychical Consequences of the Anatomical Distinction between the Sexes" (1925):

"[A] process may be set in motion which I should like to call a 'disavowal,' a process which in the mental life of children seems neither uncommon nor very dangerous but which in an adult *would mean the beginning of a psychosis*. Thus a girl may refuse to accept the fact of being castrated, may harden herself in the conviction that she does possess a penis, and may subsequently be compelled to behave as though she were a man" (p. 253, emphasis added).

We see at once that Freud introduces the notion of disavowal in connection with the sexual experience of the little girl that, in this paper, he calls the female masculinity complex. Nevertheless, in this same study, the process of disavowal is also described with regard to the little boy's sexual behavior: "[W]hen a little boy first catches sight of a girl's genital region, he begins by showing irresolution and lack of interest; he sees nothing or disavows what he has seen, he softens it down or looks about for expedients for bringing it into line with his expectations" (p. 252).

Furthermore, Freud establishes a relation between disavowal and psychosis; this defense mechanism is even held to lead to psychosis. This hypothesis refers directly to one of the themes that Freud begins to explore systematically from 1924 on (1924a,b). We find its initial arguments in "The Loss of Reality in Neurosis and Psychosis" (1924b), where disavowal bears on external reality, no longer on the reality of the absence of the penis in the mother, the little girl, the woman. Freud offers the clinical example of a girl who was in love with her brother-in-law. When her sister died, she entertained but immediately repressed the idea that he was now free to marry her. The hysterical symptoms she developed represented a neurotic reaction; a psychotic reaction would have been to disavow the fact of her sister's death.

Here Freud presents several crucial metapsychological arguments. A parallel is drawn between disavowal and repression: repression is the mechanism that leads to neurosis, disavowal to psychosis. But the contrast between disavowal and repression involves an important distinction when it comes to intrapsychic dynamics. Repression operates selectively on psychic formations that have to do with the claims of the id, whereas disavowal is a refusal of certain aspects of reality.

In this period, Freud is deeply interested in distinguishing mechanisms leading to neurosis or to psychosis. In particular, he is intent on finding in psychosis a process similar to that of repression in neurosis. For a time, the disavowal of reality seems to him to be the process he was looking for. And yet he is aware that disavowal as such is not sufficient as a differential criterion. In fact, he points out its occurrence in all subjects, if only in the form of the disavowal of castration. What makes the difference between the neuroses and the psychoses is what the disavowal bears on:

> Neurosis and psychosis differ from each other far more in that first, introductory, reaction than in the attempt at reparation which follows it.
>
> Accordingly, the initial difference is expressed thus in the final outcome: in neurosis, a piece of reality is avoided by a sort of flight, whereas in psychosis it is remodelled. Or we might say: in psychosis, the initial flight is succeeded by an active phase of remodelling; in neurosis, the initial obedience is succeeded by a deferred attempt at flight. Or again, expressed in yet another way: *neurosis does not disavow the reality, it only ignores it; psychosis disavows it and tries to replace it.* [1924b, p. 185, emphasis added]

This interest in the difference between the neuroses and the psychoses leads Freud to examine the problematics of disavowal more closely, and here a new look at the perversions enables him to extend his theorization in a remarkable way. His analysis of fetishism (1927) puts to the test several crucial metapsychological assumptions about the perversions, continuing the arguments on the disavowal of reality that he had advanced in the papers "Neurosis and Psychosis" and "The Loss of Reality" (1924a,b). Contrary to what he had first believed, the disavowal of reality is not specific to psychosis, since a perversion like fetishism illustrates it in an exemplary way. Freud also associates the disavowal of reality with another metapsychological process, the splitting of the ego, that will once again bring him back to the problematics of psychosis.

In the case of fetishism, the disavowal of reality bears selectively on the absence of the penis in the mother (the woman). Here we are once again dealing with the general question of the disavowal of castration that Freud had anticipated in his theories of infantile sexuality. In fetishism, this attitude prevails, confirming the hypothesis of the persistence of the partial drives (see Chapter 4) in regression to, and fixation at, a stage of infantile sexual development.

In a perversion like fetishism, Freud locates disavowal in the forefront of the psychic economy: the fetish is the substitute for the woman's phallus that the child believed in and was unwilling to give up. In other words, Freud is presenting a defense mechanism developed with regard to a perceived reality as a process constitutive of perverse organization, one that is able to ward off the castration anxiety directly connected to the perception of this reality: "What happened, therefore, was that the boy refused to take cognizance of the fact of his having perceived that a woman does not possess a penis. No, that could not be true: for if a woman had been castrated, then his own possession of a penis was in danger; and against that there rose in rebellion the portion of his narcissism which Nature has, as a precaution, attached to that particular organ" (1927, pp. 152–153).

Freud is now in a position to explain the link between disavowal and repression, at the same time that he differentiates them: "The oldest word in our psycho-analytic terminology, 'repression,' already relates to this pathological process. If we wanted to differentiate more sharply between the vicissitude of the *idea* as distinct from that of the *affect*, and reserve the word *Verdrängung* [repression] for the affect, then the correct German word for the vicissitude of the idea would be *Verleugnung* [disavowal]" (p. 153, emphasis in original).

Thus the instinctual process is primarily located in that of denial. A drive can be recognized by the subject only insofar as it is sustained by a representation. Since the representative of the drive is a twofold entity, the representative / representation associated with a quantum of affect, it is on the representative / representation that disavowal must bear selectively in the case of fetishism. In this case, what we are dealing with is a representative movement that refuses the lack of the penis in the mother / woman. But, at the same time, there persists a representation radically inconsistent with the former one; here this lack is acknowledged along with the castration anxiety associated with it. Disavowal, specifically centered on the reality of castration in fetishism, thus brings about an attitude that contradicts the awareness of reality.

As a result, the relation to the fetish object is a compromise formation intervening between two conflictual psychic forces:

In the conflict between the weight of the unwelcome perception and the force of [the fetishist's] counter-wish, a compromise has been reached, as is only possible under the dominance of the unconscious laws of thought—the primary processes. Yes, in his mind the woman *has* got a penis, in spite of everything, but this penis is no longer the same as it was before. Something else has taken its place, has been appointed its substitute, as it were, and now inherits the interest which was formerly directed to its predecessor. [p. 154]

In "An Outline of Psycho-analysis" (1939) Freud formulates in more detail the function of disavowal in fetishism:

This abnormality, which may be counted as one of the perversions, is, as is well known, based on the patient (who is almost always male) not recognizing the fact that females have no penis—a fact which is extremely undesirable to him since it is a proof of the possibility of his being castrated himself. He therefore disavows his own sense-perception which showed him that the female genitals lack a penis and holds fast to the contrary conviction. The disavowed perception does not, however, remain entirely without influence for, in spite of everything, he has not the courage to assert that he actually saw a penis. He takes hold of something else instead—a part of the body or some other object—and assigns it the role of the penis which he cannot do without. It is usually something that he in fact saw at the moment at which he saw the female genitals, or it is something that can suitably serve as a symbolic substitute for the penis. . . . [This process] is a compromise formed with the help of displacement, such as we have been familiar with in dreams. But our observations show us still more. The creation of the fetish was due to an intention to destroy the evidence for the possibility of castration, so that the fear of castration could be avoided. If females, like other living creatures, possess a penis, there is no need to tremble for the continued possession of one's own penis. [pp. 202–203]

In the same work, Freud emphasizes another, extremely important, metapsychological aspect of fetishism: the psychic splitting of the subject. Beginning with his 1927 study of fetishism, he had begun to note this splitting, in which the psychic apparatus contains two irreconcilable representations where the woman's castration is concerned. Once again it is in connection with the neuroses and the psychoses that he explores this hypotheses of psychic cleavage. Splitting no longer appears as a process confined to fetishism, as it is clearly evident in psychotics and neurotics as well. The hypothesis will be borne out in his later researches, achieving its final formulation in the *Outline*. Here, in the context of the disavowal of reality, Freud speaks of splitting in psychotic states: "Two psychical attitudes have been formed instead of a single one—one, the normal one, which takes account of reality, and another which under the influence of the instincts detaches the ego from reality" (p. 202).

In this sense, psychic splitting becomes a splitting of the ego, since it is within the ego that there exist two opposite attitudes with regard to external reality. Thus Freud is able to generalize as follows: "The view which postulates that in all psychoses there is a splitting of the ego could not call for so much notice if it did not turn out to apply to other states more like the neuroses and, finally, to the neuroses themselves. I first became convinced of this in cases of fetishism" (p. 202). With such an extension of the process of splitting, some of Freud's commentators have seen in this new metapsychological elaboration the beginnings of a third structural theory of the psychic apparatus.

Psychic splitting raises a final issue that touches directly on the perversions. The fetishist's disavowal of the reality of castration shows beyond a doubt how, as Freud observes in the *Outline*, two attitudes can persist for a lifetime without influencing one another. But he was well aware that this twofold attitude regarding castration is also to be found in nonfetishistic subjects. Although he does not clearly explain who these subjects might be, we have reason to think that he is referring to perverts in general. This would explain a point raised earlier on: although perversion in the adult is the continuance of one or more features of infantile polymorphous perversion, this does not in any way prevent the sexual process from finding solutions elsewhere for gratification on the level of "normal behavior." Perversion cannot be attributed solely to a fixation of sexual development at an infantile stage. We can accept the idea that this development has also reached the goal Freud described as the genital stage, where the different partial instincts are integrated.

In the *Outline*, Freud sets out from the concept of ego splitting to propose several additional arguments. These enable us to understand why fetishism is for the most part partially developed; as Freud puts it, fetishism does not entirely determine object choice and allows for more or less "normal" sexual behavior. This persistence of "normal" sexuality alongside perversion is explained by the splitting of the ego. To say that there coexist two psychic contents that do not influence one another amounts to saying that the pervert does not wholly detach his ego from external reality.

The representation that acknowledges the woman's lack of a penis promotes sexual development toward a genital stage, as with the neurotic. In return, this shows why perverse traits are actively present in neurotics, and, more generally, it indirectly confirms the inscription of the perverse process in "normal" sexual development:

> The facts of this splitting of the ego, which we have just described, are neither so new nor so strange as they may at first appear. It is indeed a universal characteristic of neuroses that there are present in the subject's mental life, as regards some particular behaviour, two different attitudes, contrary to each other and independent of each other. In the case of neuroses, however, one of these attitudes belongs to the ego and the contrary one, which is repressed, belongs to the id. *The difference*

> *between this case and the other . . . is essentially a topographical or*
> *structural one, and it is not always easy to decide with which of the*
> *two possibilities one is dealing.* [1939, p. 204, emphasis added]

It is of great interest to note the degree to which Freud insists that the radical distinction between the perversions and the neuroses presupposes a topographical and structural difference. This clarification provides some support for a structural approach to Freud's work, and, beyond that, removes the ambiguity of a formula like "neurosis is the negative of perversion."

When Freud introduces the idea of a topographic difference, this can only refer to a topography of the psychic apparatus, that is, a topography that is intrasystemic and intersystemic at the same time. In neurosis, we are dealing with an intersystemic topography, since incompatible representations are located between the ego and the id. In fetishism and the perversions in general, we are in an intrasystemic topography where the incompatible representations are found within the same system. In the first case, the defensive process at work is repression; in the second, disavowal.

In both cases we encounter the strategy of "I'm well aware, . . . but nevertheless" so subtly analyzed by Octave Mannoni (1969): the fetishist knows perfectly well that women do not have the phallus, but, unlike the neurotic, he cannot add "and yet" because the "and yet" for him is the fetish. He cannot articulate the thought that women do so have the phallus but must express the "and yet" in another way, through the mechanism of *Verleugnung*, disavowal. The disavowal in connection with the maternal phallus serves as the origin of all other denials of reality.

From the disavowal of reality, of castration, to the splitting of the ego it is as though, in the perversions, subjects manage to sustain this psychic paradox that consists in knowing something about castration even as they want to know nothing about it. In this sense, the perversions introduce us not only to infantile sexuality but to the wider question of sexual difference.

The disavowal of castration and the associated splitting directly inscribe the organization of the perverse process in the problematics of the phallus. This is the level at which we must now examine the perversions and try to define the basic elements of a structural framework. It is a crucial issue, since what is at stake in phallic problematics will explain perverse identification, the anchoring point of the structure of the perversions.

9

Phallic Identification and Perverse Identification

The problem of the anchoring point of the perverse choice must be approached in the context of the phallic logic activated in the oedipal dialectic (for the details of this dialectic, see Dor 1985, Ch. 12 and 13). This anchoring point, as we shall see, represents a special adhesion to the dimension of desire and castration, one that explains the "limit strategy" that the pervert deploys with regard to the law and symbolization.

This logic has to do with the attribution of the phallic signifier in the economy of the subject's desire. In defining the metapsychological mechanism that underlies the establishing of the perverse process, we must understand its origin in what is usually called pregenital identification.

Above all, pregenital identification is phallic insofar as it is identification with the maternal phallus. What we are dealing with here is a preoedipal identificatory experience on the part of the child, in which the dynamic of his own desire leads him to set himself up as the sole and unique object of his mother's. This dynamic stems from the first experiences of satisfaction, where the child is the object of an essential subordination. For in fact he is dependent on the mother's semantic universe, on the maternal signifiers that constitute the expression of her desire. Hence the child becomes the imaginary captive of maternal omnipotence. The mother is already omnipotent in the sense that she provides satisfaction of the child's needs, but especially because she assures the child of a supply of *jouissance* beyond the satisfaction of his needs in the strict sense.

Because of this twofold influence, the mother comes to occupy the place of the Other for the child, not only as symbolic referent in Lacan's sense of the companion of language or the treasury of signifiers, but also as the one who sets in motion a *jouissance* that, for the child, originally arises in an unmediated way, that is, without having been asked for or even sought or expected. This double psychic experience that assigns the mother the place of the Other obliges the child to apprehend maternal desire as the mainstay of his own identification. Thus the child's desire readily becomes desire for the desire of the Other, who is experienced initially as an omnipotent Other and later as a lacking Other. And it is to the extent that the Other presents herself as lacking that the child can locate his desire within a dialectic in which he identifies himself with the object that is able to fill the lack in the Other. Thus the basis of preoedipal identification, as phallic identification, is identification with the object that fills the lack in the Other.

As long as the mother embodies the Other in his dynamic of desire, the child remains captive to his phallic identification and imaginarily protected from what might challenge the omnipotence he has blindly ascribed to the mother. In this sense, he continues to be fully committed to the idea that maternal self-sufficiency is the sole dimension that legislates the order of desire. The question of sexual difference is bracketed for a time (cf. Aulagnier 1967b, p. 17).

However, the illusion of self-sufficiency cannot withstand the reality of this difference, which finally causes the child to sense that the object of his mother's desire extends beyond him. Like it or not, the child must confront a maternal desire other than her desire for him. The child's imagination spontaneously leads him to deny this "other" desire on his mother's part—that is, to deny that the mother is lacking—precisely to the extent that, sensing the lack in the other, he persists in the illusory conviction that he himself is the object that can fill this lack.

The imaginary certainty of the child's phallic identification thus inevitably comes up against an order of reality that constantly puts it in question. This challenge comes about through the intrusion of the paternal figure, whose incarnation has the task of revealing a new universe of *jouissance*. The child discovers this not only as a universe of *jouissance* that is entirely strange to him, but also as one that is forbidden, in that he believes himself to be totally excluded from it. The wavering of his original certainty is the beginning of a new knowledge of the desire of the Other and hence a new knowledge of his own. In this way the child is introduced to the stakes that come into play around sexual difference and thus to the register of castration. The entire oedipal dynamic revolves around the assumption of sexual difference through the intervention of the paternal figure as mediator of desire.

When we recognize the primary role of mediation in the paternal function, we implicitly acknowledge its influence as a vector in the economy of the child's desire as far as the phallus is concerned. Yet the paternal function operates only if it is invested with the status of mediating symbolic agency. Thus it is supported not only by the father insofar as he is present, but especially by the father promoted to the rank of symbolic father. This promotion entails Lacan's clear distinction of the paternal trilogy: the real father, the imaginary father, and the symbolic father.

The real father is the father in the reality of his being. Whether or not he is the biological father, he is still a father in the here and now of his history. But it is never in this contingent dimension of the here and now that he intervenes in the oedipal dynamic. He does so, for the child, only in the guise of imaginary father. We must understand the imaginary father in the sense of the term *imago* introduced by Jung (1911) and taken up by Freud. For the father is never psychically apprehended by the child except in the form of this paternal image, that is to say as the child has an interest in seeing him in the economy of his desire and through the way the mother speaks of him. The father is a pole of the mother's signifying projections and, at the same time, a pole of the child's personal projections. This is why his presence to the child is always much more that of the imaginary father than that of the real father. And it is with this illusionary nature that he intervenes in the oedipal dynamic. The symbolic father, for his part, intervenes structurally in the Oedipus complex as a purely signifying factor with regard to the phallic attribution.

Thus, if we are to approach the question of the father in the Oedipus complex, we must always locate the problematics of the child's desire in terms of either the imaginary or the symbolic father. This means that the onset and development of the Oedipus are inscribed outside the domain of reality. The required trajectory that the child follows in the matter of sexual difference remains imaginary, at least until he reaches the point of the symbolization of castration and of the law.

This fact of psychic reality has an major clinical implication. As it happens, the real father tends to appear as a secondary factor in the course of the Oedipus, in ambiguous expressions such as "paternal presence" or "paternal deficiency." As far as the real father is concerned, these attributes are unimportant, since what matters above all is the presence or deficiency of the imaginary father and hence, a fortiori, of the symbolic one. Everyday clinical experience shows us perfectly structured oedipal development without the presence of the real father, whether he is absent or has disappeared. On the other hand, in such cases the imaginary father and the symbolic father must be kept present through a signifying requirement that the child be genuinely confronted with the paternal function. Even the mother's discourse can fulfill this mission if the signifying requirement not only constitutes the imaginary father but, at the right moment, consecrates him in his symbolic role. In other words, the father intervenes as a structuring figure only to the extent that his word is signified in the mother's discourse as a third agency mediating the desire of the Other. As Lacan (1957–1958) puts it, "In the close connection of this maternal reference to a law that is not hers, and the fact that in reality the object of her desire is 'sovereignly' possessed by this same 'other' to whose law she refers, we have the key to the oedipal relation and to what constitutes the essential, decisive nature of this relation of the mother, as I ask you to isolate it as a relation *not to the father but to the father's word* [parole]" (seminar of January 22, 1958, emphasis added).

And Lacan (1957b) continues elsewhere: "But what I do wish to insist on is that we should concern ourselves not only with the way in which the mother accommodates herself to the person of the father, but also with *the way she takes his speech, the word* (mot), *let us say, of his authority*" (p. 218, emphasis added).

Without constant vigilance in the distinction among the real father, the symbolic father, and the imaginary father, the Oedipus remains largely unintelligible and resistant to therapeutic intervention.

Thus it is essentially in the imaginary mode that the child encounters the father as what disturbs the assurance of his phallic identification. This wavering is not only a factual one; it appears as the challenging element solely because the child senses in the mother's discourse that she is signified there as the potential object of the father's desire. Nevertheless, the child immediately performs a signifying reinterpretation of this idea, one that tends to conceal, if only temporarily, the fact that it is the mother who desires the father. On the imaginary terrain of a struggle for prestige, the child is quick to form the conviction that the father is now invested with the status of object of the mother's desire, that is, the status of the phallus that competes with him where she is concerned: "On this level, the question is 'to be or not to be' the phallus" (Lacan 1957–1958, seminar of January 22, 1958).

Phallic rivalry, then, both prompts and sustains the uncertainty of phallic identification. Hence the importance of the signifying messages at this critical time, for it is through signifiers that the child expects and perceives the reference points enabling him to orient his desire so that it can be deployed toward another horizon, or, alternately, in a direction that is closed off, obstructed, for lack of consistent signifiers to further his investigation of sexual difference.

More than ever, in this phase of the Oedipus, the structuring function of signifiers takes on a dynamic and catalytic role. In a certain way, it is because the mother's signifying discourse leaves in suspense the child's question as to her desire that this question returns back on the child, motivating him to pursue his interrogation beyond the place where his phallic identification comes to a stop. Thus the mother's discourse gives the child a "second wind" that enables him to project toward an even more enigmatic horizon what he already unknowingly senses about the order of castration and the law. The child is mobilized toward an "elsewhere" that frees him from the unmediated desire that he is negotiating with the mother in rivalry with the father.

As soon as this "second wind" finds the least cause for interruption, the dynamic tends toward a state in which entropy is stronger than the psychic effort the child must make to combat it. The suspension that takes place with regard to the wavering of phallic identification is apt to fixate a particular mode of desire reflecting a perverse identification that can later bring about the perverse structure itself.

Perverse identification and the associated structural organization crystallize around a number of indices, expressive of the stakes of desire, that will later appear as characteristics of the perverse structure. And so, once again, we must clearly explain certain metapsychological connections at work in the actualization of the perverse process.

10

The Anchoring Point of the Perversions and the Actualization of the Perverse Process

According to Freud (1923), the perverse process begins with the attribution of the phallus to the mother as she intervenes in the course of the Oedipus. This attribution is one of the solutions the child works out to the enigma of sexual difference. It is based on a fantasmatic construction that belongs to the register of infantile sexual theories. Strictly speaking, the phallic attribution involves a concept of something that should have been there and is experienced as missing. The child spontaneously constructs such a purely imaginary phallic object, and castration becomes irreducibly linked to the imaginary dimension of the phallus and not to the presence or absence of the organ, the penis.

The child is unwilling to give up the representation of the phallic mother. For him, this renunciation would mean being abruptly confronted with the real of sexual difference. The child has no psychic interest in welcoming this real as such, which would mean accepting an unbearable conclusion: freeing himself from his imaginary phallic identification and hence from his status as the sole and unique object of his mother's desire.

The orientation of his desire toward the desire of the Other entails protecting himself in fantasy by imagining an object that is presumed to be missing. This imaginary construction then leads to a way of understanding sexual difference that is set up as an alternative: to be castrated or not to be castrated. Freud rightly explains that this fantasy inevitably makes the child anxious when encountering castration and lends credence to the castration threat. The child may well become castrated or may, like the mother, have been so at one time.

Under these conditions, the emergence of castration anxiety can give rise to defensive reactions serving to neutralize it. These not only indicate refusal to accept sexual difference but also point to the psychic effort mobilized early on to evade castration. If they persist, such defensive processes orient the psychic economy along structurally typical pathways.

Let us briefly recall that Freud distinguishes three possible outcomes of castration anxiety. In one of these, the subject, like it or not, accepts the dictates of castration and submits to the law, but at the risk of experiencing an unending symptomatic nostalgia for what was lost. This is the fate of neurotics (hysterics and obsessionals). Two other outcomes are offered to subjects who do not accept castration except on condition that they may constantly transgress against it. It is in the nature of the perverse process to enter upon this uncomfortable path.

From the Freudian perspective, therefore, the perverse organization has its roots in castration anxiety and the permanent mobilization of defenses against it. Freud points to two characteristic defensive operations, fixation (associated with regression) and disavowal of reality, which occur in the organization of the perverse scenarios of homosexuality and fetishism, respectively.

Homosexuality is said to represent a narcissistic defense against castration, a defense in which the child fixes on the representation of a woman who has a penis. This representation remains actively present in the unconscious and influences the whole of later libidinal development. As Freud observes in his paper "On the Sexual Theories of Children" (1908a), if the representation of the woman with a penis becomes fixed in such a way that, when the child grows up, he cannot give up the penis in his sexual object, he will become a homosexual and seek men who remind him of women. Real women will not be possible sexual objects, since they do not have what he needs in order to be aroused. Their genitals, perceived as mutilated, cause castration anxiety and lead to horror instead of pleasure.

Fetishism involves a more complex defensive process, one that is based in the disavowal of reality. The subject refuses to acknowledge the actual existence of a traumatizing perception: the absence of a penis in the mother and women in general. This defensive strategy is associated with the elaboration of a substitute formation. It begins with the disavowal of reality that maintains a wholly infantile attitude vis-à-vis the absence of a penis in women. But, in contrast to the homosexual strategy, the fixation of the representation of the phallic mother is more labile and permits a compromise. If the woman has no penis in reality, the fetishist will create the presumably missing object by substituting another piece of reality (Freud 1927). The fetish object thus reinforces several defensive operations. It enables the subject to continue believing in the presence of the phallus, and it banishes castration anxiety. Finally, it allows the subject to choose a woman as a possible sexual object, since she is presumed to have the phallus. Ultimately, this defensive strategy circumvents libidinal engagement in the direction of homosexuality as much as it avoids it.

Starting with his work on fetishism, Freud gradually came to discern a final element that would turn out to be of major importance in the understanding of the perverse process: the splitting of the ego (see Ch. 8). Paradoxically, the fetishist is able to maintain simultaneously two intrapsychic components that at first seem incompatible: acknowledgment of the absence of the penis in women and the disavowal of this acknowledgment. In other words, reality is denied on the basis of absence, while the establishment of a fetish object is the very proof of the permanent recognition of this absence. In connection with these two contradictory psychic contents, Freud observes that they exist in the psyche without ever exerting any influence on one another. Hence he posits a psychic splitting that turns out to be an intrinsic structural feature of the subject.

This brief reminder of Freud's account of the perverse process can now be refocused in the light of the child's desire suspended at a particular moment: the wavering of his initial phallic identification because of the intrusion of the imaginary father figure, fantasized as a phallic competitor with regard to the mother. When he discovers a phallic rival, the child also perceives two orders of reality that, from then on, will complicate the course of his desire. First, he notices that his mother's desire is not exclusively dependent on his own person. And then he discovers that his mother is lacking, in no way fulfilled by himself as identified with the phallus that is the object of her desire. This double event, permanently inscribing the father in the register of imaginary phallic rivalry, gives rise to two typical structural traits: defiance and its inseparable complement, transgression, to which we shall return later on. As we have seen, the paternal figure opens up the possibility of a new world of *jouissance*, alien but also, because the child feels excluded, forbidden.

This feeling, in which the child senses the irreducible order of castration, inaugurates a new knowledge about the desire of the Other, one that orients the potential shift of his desire and the stakes of *jouissance* associated with it. Although this stasis of desire is inevitable as the Oedipus evolves, it is nonetheless crucial, because here is where the perverse structure is centered. By remaining captive within this stasis of desire, the child is vulnerable to fixation at a particular attitude regarding the phallic function. Indeed, this important moment is a fulcrum on which he will or will not tip over into a later stage favorable to his economy of desire: the acceptance of castration. This acceptance is what the pervert continues to struggle against without ever becoming actively involved in it, in other words, without ever being able to accept the losing side that can be precisely described as a lack of winning. Only this dynamic movement is able to propel the subject toward the acknowledgment of the real of sexual difference based on the lack of desire, and to lead him to accept this difference as something that can be symbolized and not as a matter of all or nothing.

The pervert avoids this fulcrum by enclosing himself within the representation of a lack that cannot be symbolized. This alienates him and thereby condemns him to an eternal challenge, the Sisyphean task of disavowing the mother's castration. Thus the future pervert is debarred from the possibility of easily accepting the symbolic castration whose function is to establish the real of sexual difference as the cause of the subject's desire. The lack signified by the intrusion of the father has the sole purpose of directing desire toward a possible new tendency.

Beyond what is at stake in perversion, this fulcrum always inaugurates what will become the signifier of the lack in the Other. The child's growing awareness of the dimension of the symbolic father is supported by a psychic "pre-sentiment" that he will have to confront if he is to give up his representation of the imaginary father. But the father cannot lose his role of phallic rival without the intervention of this signifier of the lack in the Other that invites the child to abandon the register of *being* (being the phallus) for the register of *having* (having it). The transition from being to having is therefore possible only insofar as the father appears to the child to be the one who is presumed to possess the phallus that the mother desires. This phallic attribution, investing the father with the rank of symbolic father, confers on him the authority of representative of the law. In this exclusive capacity, the mediation of the prohibition of incest has a structuring function for the child.

In certain ways, the shadow of the symbolic father remains exactly this mediating role, a role that the pervert wishes to ignore because it requires him to acknowledge the lack in the Other. Through this repeated disavowal of lack, the pervert enters into a conspiracy by subscribing to the contradiction that we have mentioned. Since the paternal intrusion leads the child to believe that the lacking mother desires the father only because he is not without the phallus, then all the child has to do is provide her with it in imagination, and to sustain this attribution, to neutralize sexual difference and the lack that it makes obvious.

Permanently disavowing sexual difference amounts to positing unisexuality. But, conversely, positing unisexuality implies that the pervert is always challenging, even while recognizing, the law of the father that decisively governs the dynamics of desire. This paradoxical confusion tends to become the sole mode of functioning with regard to desire. The absence of the maternal (and female) penis comes to represent danger, a fantasmatic horror of the repetition, in his own case, of the castration supposedly performed on the mother by the father. Impeding the mobilization of the subject's desire toward a new stage, this fantasy makes him renounce the assumption of his own desire, beyond castration.

This blindness results in a confusion between giving up desire and giving up the primal object of his desire. What blocks his assumption of desire is, above all, the defensive system that makes him unable to discover what he should have discovered: that only the renunciation of the primal object of desire safeguards the possibility of desire itself, by giving it the new status that comes with the paternal mediation, a status that authorizes the right to desire (cf. Aulagnier 1967b) as desire for the desire of the other. Because of his particular psychic dynamics, therefore, the pervert remains trapped in an untenable economy of desire that deprives him of this right. He wears himself out negotiating this psychic situation, constantly trying to *demonstrate* that the only law he acknowledges is the imperative law of his own desire and not the law of the desire of the other. All the ravages of the perverse process stem from this testing.

The disavowal basically involves the mother's desire for the father, in other words, the issue of sexual difference as such, and this is why the pervert, more than anyone else, is condemned to endure the torment of castration horror. This being the case, he must preserve a relation to the mother, and to women in general, that is stereotypically symptomatic. Nevertheless, this disavowal could not be sustained unless the pervert recognized the mother's desire for the father, if only to make it the object of his disavowal. On one level, he does indeed know something about sexual difference, though he uses up most of his energy in rejecting its primary implication, namely that this difference is the signifying cause of desire. In constantly striving to keep alive the possibility of a *jouissance* that would get free of this signifying cause, the pervert has no recourse but to subscribe to the defiance of the law and to its transgression. These are some of the most fundamental features of the perverse structure, and we shall now take a closer look at them.

11

The Horror of Castration and the Relation to Women. Defiance and Transgression

The child's acknowledgment of the symbolic father is directly dependent on attributing the phallus to him. And yet it is not because the child knows that the father has a penis that he necessarily makes this attribution. Beyond anatomy, the child can presuppose the possession of the phallus only if, as Lacan notes, he discovers that the father has managed to become preferred by the mother by becoming the object of her desire. This libidinal investment suggests to the child that he is no longer the site of the mother's *jouissance*. But, in addition, the orientation of the mother's desire toward the father teaches the child that what the father desires in the mother is her difference from him. Sexual difference becomes the signifier of desire, the indispensable support for the symbolization of lack.

The pervert, maintaining both an awareness of sexual difference and a simultaneous rejection of it, is trapped in the impossibility of assuming this lack symbolically. To put it more precisely, while recognizing this difference he rejects its implications. Now, beyond the fact that the mother does not have a penis, the crucial implication is, above all, not having the object of desire. She is invested as the locus of the omnipotence of desire only insofar as the father has something that can make her desire. This is the logical implication of sexual difference as signifying cause of desire. In regard to it, the pervert acts as though, having become aware of its full scope, he prefers the possibility of a *jouissance* that could evade it. Such a *jouissance* can be imagined only through a fantasmatic construct elaborated around material from infantile sexual theories, a construct that perpetuates the horror experienced in the face of sexual difference. The horror of castration is especially active in all perverts because it is perpetuated by the fantasy of a real castration.

The pervert's drama of castration horror has its permanent energy source in a complex dialectic involving two series of imaginary psychic productions, the first having to do with the mother's castration and the second, closely connected with it, having to do with her desire for the father, or, more generally, with her desire as such. For the pervert, this interconnection leads to a constant oscillation between two potentialities that neutralize the dynamic of his own desire. To begin with, the pervert is convinced that the mother has no penis because she was castrated by the father; the father is thus responsible for the horror of a castration that is believed to be real. Then the father is held to be the agent responsible for making the mother compromise herself, constraining her in the unjust law that says that the desire of one person is always subject to the desire of the other. Thus the mother is believed to be deprived of her presumed control over the omnipotence of desire (cf. Aulagnier 1967b, p. 22).

But an additional fantasmatic element enters into the perverse construct, and this is the belief that the mother was wrong to have compromised herself by desiring the father's desire. This accusation projected onto the mother enables the pervert to maintain the belief that she was complicit in her own castration: the horror of castration would not exist if the mother's desire hadn't led to her deliberate collusion with the father. Thus the pervert can take comfort in the fantasy of a father who might not be castratable and hence in the possibility that he himself might not be castrated (here again, see Aulagnier 1967b, p. 22). The castration horror entailed by this twofold fantasmatic option, constantly recalling as it does the order of lack, brings about a situation in which the pervert can find no outlet for *jouissance* except through a compromise. In reaction to this horror, all he can do is mobilize the other fantasmatic construct in which the mother is omnipotent in the realm of desire. Only the unconditional adherence to the fantasy of a mother who is not lacking can counteract the father's influence by positing that he is no longer what the mother desires. The pervert can henceforth continue to act as the sole and unique object of desire that brings *jouissance* to the mother.

It is easy to understand how this fantasmatic compromise to which the pervert clings inevitably determines certain aspects of psychic functioning and the especially stereotyped way in which they are expressed, not only in the pervert's relation to the law but, more generally, in the interpellation of his desire by women and men.

We now have to consider what leads the child, early on, to seek the protective armor of this fantasy that makes him unable to assume the castration he dreads. Clinical experience sheds considerable light on this issue.

To the extent that we can speak of an anchoring point for the perverse process, we are referring to certain precipitating factors that intervene at the crucial moment when the child questions the certainty of his phallic identification. To return to the ambiguity mentioned in Chapter 9, it seems clear that equivocation conjointly promoted by the parents with regard to this questioning leads to the loss of phallic identification in favor of the perverse kind. The equivocation involves the libidinal complicity of the mother and the silent collusion of the father.

The libidinal complicity of the mother occurs on the level of seduction. It is important to understand that this seduction is actually undertaken in reality and is not just the result of the child's fantasmatic excesses. Most of the time, what we see clinically is the mother's libidinal appeal to the erotic needs of her child. In return, the child can only welcome the mother's responses as evidence of her recognition and encouragement of his erotic impulses toward her (cf. Aulagnier 1967b, p. 24).

At the decisive moment of the Oedipus, this seductive appeal of the mother's, which occurs in the form of showing, intimating, and touching, is truly tormenting to the child. In fact, while the child sees here an actual incentive to *jouissance*, the mother is usually silent on the meaning of the father's intrusion and its underlying question of desire. In her erotic complicity with the child, the latter can deceive himself about the absence of paternal mediation with regard to the mother's desire. Yet the father is an intruder all the same, and he remains one all the more so because the mother, by not confirming her desire for him, never removes it from the realm of possibility for the child. The father's role can only be experienced as troubling and enigmatic. The signifying suspension of the issue of the mother's desire perpetuates the ambiguity that excites the child's libidinal activity. And so he will try to seduce the object of his *jouissance* still further, in the hope of removing any doubt about the meaning of the father's role, confident in the mother's encouragement that invites him to belittle this role. Defiance, a highly characteristic feature of the perverse structure, finds its most powerful source in this appeal to derision.

And such derision is most often encouraged by the mother's implicit silence. Although she may refer to the father's role in mediating her desire in order to counteract the child's erotic investment in her, the child never fails to notice her inconsistency and dishonesty as she expresses her reservations in the form of a bogus threat or interdiction. Thus he remains doubly captive: in her seductiveness and in the her make-believe prohibition. It does not take much more to give him to understand that he is being invited to transgression.

But this kind of ambiguity on the mother's part does not have a decisive influence unless it is echoed and confirmed by the tacit collusion of a father who is willing to be deprived of his symbolic rights, to let the mother take over his word with all the ambiguity that this delegation implies. This does not mean that the father's word is accorded no value, as is the case in certain prepsychotic family constellations. In the case of the perversions, the child is not subordinated to a maternal law that does not refer to the law of the father. The pervert's mother does not "lay down the law" to the father, unlike the psychotic's "out-law" mother, as Lacan calls her. The child does remain confronted with the dimension of a desire referred to the Name-of-the-Father, that is, subject to the law of the desire of the other. At the very most, we can say that its meaning, as he apprehends it, is not fundamentally carried by the word of the father to which the mother submits. It is in this way that the father's silent collusion reinforces the ambiguity by authorizing the mother's discourse to represent the prohibition. But it is also true that, because of this delegation, the child nevertheless receives a prohibition referred to the law of the father, even if it is uttered by the mother, and this saves him from a psychotic outcome.

Still, the collusiveness of this delegation confuses the child, trapping him within an irremediable ambiguity. On the one hand, there is the threatening and prohibiting mother who conveys the father's symbolic word, and on the other hand there is the seductive mother who encourages the child to bring her *jouissance* and mocks the structuring signification of the father's law.

The opposite side of the coin of this tacit delegation on the part of the complicit father is often a fixed adherence to regulations. While failing to orient the oedipal dialectic by unequivocally signifying the locus and the cause of the mother's *jouissance*, the father displaces this summons to the child onto the dictates of rules. Obviously, the more totalitarian this rigor, the more the child is convinced of the father's inconsistency and symbolic fragility. As we might expect, it is primarily in the register of what one might call phallic education that the strictness of such fathers is most evident. Pedagogical injunctions rain down all the harder so that the child or adolescent will learn "to be a man." Most of the time these precepts emphasize imaginary stereotypes of masculinity so strongly because they serve to mask these fathers' own phallic ambivalence in the face of castration.

The alienation of the child in the intrigue of the mother's seduction and the symbolic negligence of the father leads him to confirm the fantasy of an all-powerful mother, the phallic mother he will not renounce. The image of this phallic mother will accompany him relentlessly each time he formulates a strategy of desire toward women, nor will he renounce these women either, even if this sometimes means seeking to meet them in the person of other men.

Haunted by the fantasy of the phallic mother, the pervert is condemned in advance to maintain an economy of desire with regard to women that is, if not impossible, at least torturing. Each woman incarnates and is parasited by a representation of Janus-faced womanhood, thereby revealing the structurally ambiguous relation of perverse desire to the desire of the other. Every representation of woman necessarily reminds the pervert of a set of stigmata unconsciously inscribed as the marks of his subjection to the double fantasy of the mother as not lacking / castrated. Although he constantly seeks appropriate specimens in reality, each woman in turn appears either as a virgin in the odor of sanctity or as a repulsive whore. These two incompatible representations are the terrain of the unconscious expression of the pervert's desire.

On the one hand, a woman can represent the completely idealized phallic mother. Such an idealization serves to keep the pervert safe from the mother as object of desire. Since this idealization is a defensive process, the woman is considered not only omnipotent but also innocent of all desire. She is a pure and perfect object, and her dazzling perfections place her beyond reach, as forbidden as she is unattainable. She thus represents the feminine ideal. Always present and selfsame, the most she can offer the pervert is the privilege of her benevolence and protection. On the other hand, the woman may also represent the repulsive and abject mother, the sexuated mother who is all the more repugnant for desiring the father and being desirable to him. The pervert can only relegate this woman / mother to the rank of whore, that is, the contaminated object offered to everyone's desire because she is not exclusively reserved for his own. This is the feminine incarnation that leads the pervert to the horror of castration. He is repelled by the castrated female genital, fantasized as a gaping and loathsome wound, but threatening also because it can injure his own penis if he gives in to desire. In all cases, the desirable and desiring woman is a dangerous figure for the pervert. She represents either a creature whom he flees because she can condemn him to an impotence unconsciously maintained by the castrative fantasy of the *vagina dentata* (see Gessain 1957), or a creature he abuses as odious, all the more deserving of mistreatment because her repugnant nature is a source of *jouissance* for him.

12

Clinical Example: Parental Ambiguity as Initiating the Perverse Process and the Horror of Castration

Despite its intentional brevity, the following clinical example[1] is an excellent illustration of the fantasmatic synergy described in the previous chapter: parental ambiguity leading to the perverse process and the horror of castration symptomatically put to the test in the erotic investment of women.

Having been a much wanted baby, and the only child for the first five years of his life, this man was the object of intense maternal adoration. He could not bear to be separated from his mother, and she took great pains to ensure that this dire eventuality would never occur. Present at all times, she succeeded in persuading a doctor to put off the boy's entry into school for two years in the name of some claims of illness that were as obscure as they were convenient.

---

1. The clinical material has been modified to protect confidentiality and is being used with the patient's consent.

The father, occupied with demanding professional activities, hardly troubled this idyllic relationship. Moreover, beyond the expectable infantile amnesia, this man retained no memory of this father from this time other than his constant absence. But he recalled quite precisely the numerous physical interactions with his mother. She would always invite him to share her bath and often undressed in his presence. Her attentions to his personal hygiene were protracted and extensive, often bordering on indecency. In the name of love, mutual caressing and touching occurred on a daily basis, and his mother used to tell him how susceptible he was to this.

When he was 6, two events disturbed this perfect relationship: the birth of a little brother and a sexual experience that would turn out in retrospect to have been traumatic.

His mother told him early on about the coming birth of the new child, somewhat as if this were a guilty betrayal. In order to repair the breach in their liaison, she constantly assured him that she would love him even more than when he was alone with her. It was at this time that she began to call him her "little man." Not a day passed without her showing him her stomach, inviting her "little man" to caress it at length. He seemed to remember that she would also caress herself at these times. The meaning of these caresses, enigmatic to say the least, would become clear only after the second of the two events.

This episode involved the arrival of a nursemaid in the home. Engaged by the mother to help her during her pregnancy, she was introduced to the child as a mother substitute who would devote herself to his every need—this as an atonement on the part of the mother for the coming intrusion of the sibling. The maid, whose job it was to devote herself to the child, soon began going beyond the limit in doing so. While his mother was away, she led him into her room, undressed him, got completely undressed herself, and caressed herself in front of the dumbfounded child. After inviting him, in the course of thorough explorations, to learn about sexual pleasure, she ended by masturbating the little boy and orally molesting him. She imposed absolute secrecy on him: if he betrayed her, the activity would never be repeated.

These interactions continued every day for several weeks. The child was quickly initiated into a whole range of erotic techniques that always left him in a confused state of delight and anxiety mixed together. But one of these scenes of seduction made him unusually anxious: the maid actually sat astride him and copulated with him.

Apparently the secret was well kept. Still, it seemed impossible to him that his mother would know nothing about it, since she had surprised him, at least once, entirely naked in the maid's room while the maid herself was in her underwear. Whatever the case, the mother never said a word. There is every reason to believe that this loveplay would have gone on for a long time, if the maid had not been sent away after a minor theft.

After her departure, the child kept after his mother, assiduously but carefully, to try to reexperience with her some of the intense feelings the maid had so often aroused in him. Yet he was very circumspect in his ardor, since the maid, in imposing silence, had initiated him into *jouissance* as a forbidden pleasure.

This prohibition made him not only exceptionally cautious in approaching his mother sexually but also, oddly enough, increasingly attentive to the presence of his father, whom he soon discovered to be a troublemaker. Symptomatically, all his memories of his father's presence seem to have begun at this time. Moreover—and this, too, is symptomatic—his father seemed to become more and more enraged and threatening every day. In fact, the father was terribly brutal and violent with his wife. But he had always been like this; the child had simply repressed it energetically while carrying on his perfect love affair with his mother. In reality, on each of his intermittent appearances in the house, the father would seize on any pretext whatsoever to strike his wife and heap verbal abuse on her. Among his insults, one of the most frequent, "Go get yourself fucked in the ass," began to intrigue the child on account of its compulsive repetition that weighed on his thoughts. Although this expression was in itself unintelligible to him at this time, it probably resonated unconsciously thanks to the expert attentions of the maid. Soon thereafter, this question was to return for him in a way that could not be avoided.

The patient recalled that he began to take advantage of his father's absences to console his mother for the abuse that was inflicted on her. She never discouraged him. These long-drawn-out scenes of consolation led to mutual fondling, during which the two of them would confide their pleasure. Although these "body to body" sessions never reached the level of debauchery of his former adventures, he recalled fleeting moments of mutual sexual investigation.

The birth of the brother disrupted this libidinal idyll. He experienced the departure of his mother for the maternity hospital as an almost conjugal abandonment. Feeling his privilege infringed on, he spent several months after her return making jealous outbursts. The father would sometimes intervene to separate the protagonists in this hellish passion, who would take this occasion to infuriate him with their claim to imaginary adulterous infidelities. As usual, some physical and verbal brutalities were the outcome of these "marital" misunderstandings between the mother and her "little man." Terrorized by the violence surrounding him, the boy surrendered under the barrage of humiliating sarcasm that his father directed against him, wounding him deeply by drumming it into him that he was afraid of everything, cried and complained like a little girl, and would never be a man.

Putting on a brave face, he got used to the idea that he was no longer the only one to enjoy the presence and the favors of his mother. Besides, since the birth of the brother she had been somewhat more reserved physically with him, though in an ambiguous way. After allowing him with obvious pleasure to caress her, she would often order him to stop on the grounds that he was too big now and his father was against it.

The law of the father, unfortunately absent in his everyday boorishness, was thus timidly evoked in the mother's discourse, but with a highly suspicious ambivalence. Though the appeal to the prohibition would always come after the furtive physical exchanges, it almost never preceded them.

Despite this captivity under the iron rule of an ambivalent mother who was both an eager seducer and a ridiculously inadequate prohibitor, the child was gradually forced, as the months and years passed, to sublimate the erotic activity he had engaged in with her into tenderness, attentiveness, and solicitude, for which his mother was always grateful. On the other hand, in the child's imagination the father only confirmed his standing as a dull-witted and evil brute. The boy gradually persuaded himself that his mother gave in to the father helplessly but did not desire him. He thus remained absolutely convinced that he was still her favored love object.

Nevertheless, certain changes began to appear in his relation to her. For her part, the mother never really gave up her interest in her many seductive undertakings toward her son. In particular, she never passed up an opportunity to appear naked in front of him, or, better still, dressed in a suggestive way that barely concealed the object of his lust. But he reacted to her solicitations with an increasing avoidance. Little by little, his mother's body became repellent to him. He came to find her genitals disgusting.

When he was about 12, he was involuntarily exposed to a violently sadistic sexual scene between his parents. Above all, he remembered having been upset not so much by the inappropriateness of what his father was trying to make his mother undergo as by the eager pleasure expressed in the mother's encouragement of him. The accidental viewing of this primal scene led to a punishment that was as memorable as it was inexplicable to the child: he was beaten with a belt by a savagely out-of-control and foulmouthed father. Overwhelmed by this parental exhibition that he did not understand, profoundly wounded by the injustice of the reprisal he had suffered, he lapsed into a state of inertia that had its predictable outcome several days later, when he experienced a demeaning sexual trauma that would turn out to be decisive for the future course of his libidinal investments.

While returning from school, he was propositioned by an unknown man of about 20. Unprotestingly, he let himself be seduced by this person, who took him to his apartment and summarily raped him. Stunned by the casualness of this sexual experience, he went home feeling not only degraded but corrupt for having given in so passively, though not without some pleasure, to painful brutality in order to satisfy someone else's *jouissance*. He solemnly promised himself never to forget this shameful memory.

Shortly thereafter, a period of torment set in. He was soon surprised to find that, without knowing why, he hated women. At first he was ambivalent: women seemed to him to be vaguely alien creatures, and he could not understand why men were attracted to them. Then he became insistent: all women were detestable and threatening and had to be avoided. At the same time, he became interested in associating with men, and his homosexual experiences began when he was 18. Though they were fairly frequent, they were always difficult, without particular attraction or pleasure, mostly ending in sordid sadomasochistic experiences.

A paradoxical interest in women followed, though he continued to feel a deep sexual disgust toward their genitals, accompanied by an ongoing fantasy of doubting the existence of the vagina. This almost obsessive uncertainty led him to detailed investigations designed to disconfirm his imaginary belief. Neither his regular visits to prostitutes, whom he paid solely in order to get visual assurance of the existence of the vagina, nor his constant attendance at pornographic movies ever managed to undo the stubborn doubt. It is clear that the persistence of this doubt was a result of fantasies about the phallic mother, the absence of the vagina in women representing a displacement of the question of the absence of the penis. If, on the level of fantasy, what is unfortunately missing in the mother / the woman is the penis and not the vagina, it is especially important that, on the level of reality, the absence has to focus on the vagina. Only the constant doubt mobilized by this absence forced him to seek regular disconfirmation in reality, through prostitutes and pornographic films. On the other hand, however, the repeated verification made it possible for him to imagine all these proofs as evidence of the phallic attribution. The vagina is always just an invaginated penis, and so the woman does indeed have it: whoever doubts this has only to go and see, and go and see again.

The most irrefutable proof of this phallic fantasy came in the course of the analysis, when therapeutic progress enabled him to have several successive relationships with women, relationships that were often difficult and that involved sexual experiences marked for a long time by anxiety and disappointing standstills. One of the obscure causes of anxiety finally yielded its meaning: the fantasied fear of losing his penis. This was the ordinary fantasy of the *vagina dentata* so often found in the clinical treatment of men, but it always takes on added resonance in the pervert, for whom it revives the fantasy of the mother who is responsible for the horror of castration.

At or about the same time, a typical discourse was elaborated around the father. At first represented as a dull-witted and violent brute, he gradually came to be seen differently as women came to be seen as more and more acceptable. Via an unconscious identification, the father was now viewed as unable to bear the horror evoked by the desire for women. His violence and brutality were imperceptibly transformed into reactions of legitimate defense. The father, not the mother, thus became the victim; he was no longer the troublemaker who imposed his unjust law on the woman (the mother) but, on the contrary, the one who was subject to the law of women.

In this reversal, we can again observe one of the favorite imaginary aspects of the perverse fantasy, namely the notion of a father who was potentially uncastratable if only the mother hadn't dragged him into the original sin of desire. The whole scenario gradually turned upside down, since now it was the father who had to be protected from the mother's mistreatment. This identificatory alliance of father and son was clearly as problematical as the antagonism it replaced. As one might expect, it did not last long. The allegory of the father as victim could only bring the patient urgently back to the initial question of the mother's desire, the crucial stakes around which the perverse structure is formed.

What happened next is what we often find when the course of the analysis brings the perverse patient right to the threshold of this question: he broke off treatment. The rupture usually occurs in a way that is typical of the intrapsychic strategies of the perverse structure, defiance and transgression. In the present case, the investigation of the mother's desire, at first disguised by a convenient displacement, was quickly recentered around the analytic frame. The patient began to challenge the frequency of his weekly sessions, defying me to impose the usual rhythm. In a second phase, the issue became the timing of the sessions, which he hoped to modify as he pleased. My firm opposition to both attempts could not be accepted, or even understood, except as an invitation to transgression.

In one of the final sessions, I had hardly ushered him into my office when he quickly seated himself in my chair, loudly stating that he had a major announcement to make. Claiming that I had been symptomatically deaf to his recent entreaties, he felt obliged to switch roles, at least for some time. Firmly settled in my chair, he ordered me to listen carefully to what he had to say, advising me that, even if I didn't want to acknowledge anything, at least my unconscious would understand:

> Firstly, having been unresponsive to his latest demands, I had to realize that I was not really there to help him with his problems, as I had presumably engaged to do.
>
> Secondly, I also had to realize that psychoanalysis was a sham if the analyst refused, without any valid justification, to be of service to patients who were experiencing these difficulties.
>
> Thirdly, I was to consider myself informed that, on account of this betrayal, he was dismissing me on the spot in favor of a colleague who guaranteed that he could be more understanding of these requests.

When he was done with these accusations, I offered him payment for the masterly brio with which he had conducted "my" analytic session. A huge outburst of laughter then put an end to the final act of this masquerade, after which I confirmed the appointment for "his" next session.

Needless to say, he did not return.

13

*The Relation to Women. Defiance.
Transgression. Differential Diagnosis
of the Perversions, Obsessional Neurosis,
and Hysteria*

In accordance with the politics" of the disavowal that controls
his psychic economy, the pervert, as we have seen, is the prisoner
of a conflict in his relations with women, who make him bend
under the yoke of castration. To escape that horror, he can only
idealize the woman as a virgin or mistreat her as a whore. This
antinomy produces several clinical manifestations that enable us
to base the diagnosis of perverse structure on distinct and typical
features. Yet this unusual mode of relating to women is not clinically relevant when it comes to the perversions unless we are very
precise about some points of differential diagnosis with neurotic
organizations like obsessional or hysterical structure.

The economy of desire in some cases of obsessional neurosis
can give rise to typical behaviors toward women that may seem
similar to those of the pervert. For example, the reverential adoration of women that some obsessionals develop seems to be based

on a kind of radical idealization, as in the perversions. The maze of rhetorical and material precautions in which certain obsessionals so easily become entangled when courting the women they desire soon becomes a true veneration that can at first look like the cult of the untouchable woman to whom the pervert pays homage.

In the clinical treatment of obsessionals, this veneration turns out to have a different logic. The logic of desire characteristic of obsessional structure has to do with putting at a distance. The obsessional is constantly trying to remain at a distance from his desire so as to know nothing about it. If the woman he desires is untouchable, this is essentially because he does not want to give himself permission to recognize that he desires her. The desired woman is not set apart as a woman free of all desire, nor is she out of reach because reaching her is impossible. If she seems forbidden, this is not intended to confirm the fantasy of the omnipotent phallic woman whose imaginary representation must be maintained. For the obsessional, the woman may be set apart as forbidden because the subject himself, under pain of feeling at risk, must forbid himself to know that he desires.

There is an additional component of obsessional logic that can be confusing with regard to the setting up of the woman as an idealized object. This is the tendency of some obsessionals to put the desired woman "in the archives" or "under glass" as a precious collector's item that must be kept untouched. Here the woman is reduced to an object of possession, only accidentally of consumption. The obsessional chooses not to touch her, the point being that she should be there, always there, eternally there.

In this mode of idealization of the woman, quite common among obsessionals, there is a remnant of infantile despotism. In particular, this aspect of infantile despotism gives free rein to the drive for mastery of the object. If the feminine object is reduced to an object that is neither desiring nor desirable, the obsessional is somehow reassured in his worry about possessing her. In other words, it is in smothering the desire of the other that the obsessional manages to sustain the logic of his own.

Unconsciously invested as a mother substitute, the woman must remain fully and completely fulfilled by the presence of the obsessional subject, who is unconsciously identified with her phallus. In this "putting on ice" of the feminine object, the obsessional maintains the compromise that governs his desire. And this putting on ice sometimes looks like imposing order or bringing her into line, with the aim of making sure that she remains as inanimate as possible, that is, nondesiring.

To accomplish this aim, the obsessional will spare no effort in setting up a cult of this sterilized object of desire, a cult that soon becomes idealization with an underlying idolatry. Now, this veneration is probably one of the worst cults that can be offered to a woman, because it tends to neutralize in advance any vague attempt on her part to desire. The adoration is primarily sustained by the obsessional's fantasy of doing everything for her, giving her everything so that she will lack nothing. He will make great sacrifices toward this end. No price is too great, as long as she does not budge, does not make any claims or demands. The woman venerated in this way is caught in the vise of an implacable logic: "a place for everything, and everything in its place." It is in this way that the obsessional pays homage to his object and most deeply cherishes her. When the other's dynamic of desire is dead, as it were, it is at this moment, and this moment alone, that the obsessional finds *jouissance*: to be precise, silent *jouissance* at the misfortune of his desire.

Obviously, the idealized woman is never completely "dead." Sooner or later, then, the obsessional will find himself in the throes of disorder when the object of the cult, untouchable (and untouched), and fixed in place, begins to move—that is, to desire and to signify herself as desirable in the gaze of the other. This is all it takes to unsettle the obsessional's supposedly stable universe. Once this unsettling begins, the object of the cult is suddenly no longer idealized. Yet she does not seem to him to be dangerous or repugnant, as she does to the pervert. On the contrary, for the obsessional it is as if he now sees her as she really is, someone who can flee, who can escape his control: someone he can lose. Hence his pathetic attempts at getting back the lost object.

In contrast to the pervert, who leaves or abuses his repulsive object, the obsessional does not know to what saint to appeal in order to be pardoned.[1] He is now the overwhelmed, guilty martyr, prepared to make any sacrifice to regain the privileges he was so sure he had won from the mummified object of desire. To get her to come back and not leave again, he may become more hysterical than a true hysteric. He is ready to pay anything, endure anything, if only things return to their previous state of deathlike order. Most important is that lack once again be neutralized and that the woman assume her role as inert object under the bell jar of his kindly asphyxiation of her desire. Only then can she again be worshipped as an ideal object.

Experience tends to show that the greatest sacrifices and the most obsequious atonements are to no avail. The fault line opened up by the surge of desire in the other, her being desired and also desirable, inevitably reminds the obsessional of loss—more exactly, of castration and the loss it involves. Here we have the crucial difference in what upsets the obsessional in contrast to the pervert. The former does not have the pervert's safety net, since he cannot take comfort in the denial of castration with which the pervert sustains his *jouissance*. The woman idealized by the obsessional is

---

1. Translator's note: In the original text there is an explicit pun on *saint* and the homonym *sein* ("breast").

so only by virtue of the magic fantasy construct that places her in this position. But such a construct is never entirely safe. The first sign of desire on the woman's part is sometimes enough to breach the rampart of this entrenched camp, forcing the obsessional to do without the symptomatic relief his neurosis had provided. At least he has to do without it temporarily, encountering castration and the lack in the other. Where the pervert never gives up the illusion of the feminine ideal he has created, the obsessional exhausts himself trying to patch up this ideal that is always just a nostalgic trace of oedipal prehistory.

Thus we can say that obsessionals behave toward the idealized woman like romantics of "being," nostalgic as they are for the phallic identification they had to trade for the discomfort of the "having" imposed by the law of the father.

Similarly, we can pinpoint certain differences between male hysteria and the perversions with regard to the relation to women. Since the hysteric's agitated behavior is richer and more highly colored than what we find in the obsessional, differential diagnosis with certain structural features of the perversions is less easy to establish. Moreover, there is often some ambiguity in view of the fact that there is an aspect of hysteria that is always more or less favorable to perverse manifestations.

The relation of the hysterical man to the female other is caught up from the outset in a certain type of representation by virtue of its very structure. Most of the time this representation is that of an idealized woman placed on an inaccessible pedestal. This is not the virgin, untouchable and undesiring, of the pervert's fantasy. Nor is she the woman worshipped by the obsessional as a sterilized object without desire. On the contrary, the woman idealized by the male hysteric is as desirable as she can be, placed on a pedestal as a precious object to be exhibited. The woman must be pitilessly seductive, available, always offered to the gaze of the fascinated and envious other. Most important is that the object never deviate from this function. When she does so, she immediately loses all her glamour and seductive attractiveness. She becomes threatening, something to be destroyed. Now hateful, she must in one way or another atone for having fallen from the pedestal.

In hysteria there is a subtle dialectic in the oscillation between the idealized exhibited woman and, on the other hand, the hateful fallen woman, who is suddenly responsible for all the evils on earth. This subtle interplay can be explained only in terms of the hysteric's ambivalent relation to the phallus.

For the hysteric, the woman is the object par excellence that enables him to orient himself with regard to the possession of the phallus. He is dramatically caught up in the problematics of the phallus on the side of "not having it." Feeling himself to be without the phallic attribute, he readily responds to the woman's desire with the implicit notion: "I don't have the penis" (impotence) or "I don't really have it" (premature ejaculation). Without going further into the penis / phallus dialectic,[2] let us note that this symptomatic confusion and the phallic stakes it presupposes enable us to understand the nature of the radical shift the hysteric makes in his representation of the woman. As a seductive and brilliant object to be exhibited, the idealized woman is fantasized as an object of phallic admiration offered to everyone's gaze. The hysteric behaves in such a way as to avoid having to know whether or not he has the phallus. In a certain sense, he has it. It is here, in the form of this idealized woman, always at his disposal and always radiant.

This explains why this woman, promoted to the phallic function, is a jealously guarded possession, offered to the limitless admiration of others. The more she is coveted by others, the more

---

2. For details, see Israël 1976, pp. 63 and 119–128, and Perrier 1978, pp. 74–78.

the hysteric is unconsciously confirmed in the belief that the phallus is coveted through him. In this sense, if the woman is an inalienable piece of property, he is guaranteed possession of the phallus.

Nevertheless, this fantasy is a fragile one. It presupposes that the woman idealized as the phallic attribute must be desirable but not too desirous. If she is, matters become complicated. The problems begin as soon as the idealized female object starts to desire her most faithful admirer, namely her hysterical partner. The woman's desire automatically brings up the question of the possession of the phallus. If she starts to desire, this proves that she lacks something, and if what she desires is the hysterical male, this presumes that he has what she lacks. But this is precisely the question that agitates him.

In such a case, the woman quickly becomes a worrisome, not to say persecutory, object who condemns him to be put to the test of the phallic attribution. His comfortable universe is shaken, and he is now subject to the panoply of symptoms that accompany sexual intercourse. At first the problems may be endurable. But true hell begins when the woman is not only seen as lacking but begins to make demands in that mode of desire that leads each one of us to run after object *a*, the object of desire. The hysterical man feels automatically disqualified in this situation. In fact he discredits himself, in advance and unknowingly, because of his symptomatic position vis-à-vis the phallus.

In this dialectic, the woman cannot help falling from the pedestal and becoming an object of hatred, all the more so because she is now shown to be an object that may be lost. In other words, for the hysteric the entire imaginary notion of property is upset in this fall, since the idealized incarnation of the phallic object is disappearing. And this is why he becomes extremely alarmed. From his point of view, the mistreatment of the fallen woman is justified. To abuse and destroy the object is unconsciously to cancel out the lack of lack in the woman. In this way it may be possible for him unconsciously to regain the possessive control of the object. Moreover, at these moments of breakdown, when the hysteric is confronted with the signifier of lack in the female other, it is highly typical for him to oscillate in an attitude of ambivalence. This is the ambivalence that he always experiences toward the phallus. He may choose in turn to be hostile or to make atonement, but the point remains to assure himself of mastery over the object. But if he becomes ostentatiously aggressive, as is sometimes the case, he is very soon overwhelmed by his own destructive undertaking.

Most of the time, this leads him to make a rapid about-face in the direction of repentance. The expiatory shift takes on an almost magical air, since it is designed to regain the good graces of the mistreated woman. To this end, the hysteric is likely to give his all. Taking advantage of the logic belonging to his structure, he willingly places his desire in the service of the other, the female other he is so eager to restore to the pedestal from which she has fallen. In a situation of atonement in which forgiveness can admit no compromise, the hysteric is more than ready to offer himself as the unforgivable victim, prepared to sacrifice everything on the altar of his idealized object. Since the benefits of humiliation are as wished for as they are expected, the atonement is without limit so as—unconsciously—to sanctify the intolerable narcissistic wound. He presents himself as the ultimate unworthy one in the face of the fantasized disaster occasioned by the vanishing of the phallic object. This unworthiness is all the more precious because it is the visible sign of the misery of not having it in the eyes of the woman who can repair that deficit. The sacrifice must therefore be carried as far as possible.

In any event, what we are dealing with in the hysterical man is a tragic confusion between love and desire. It is as though love has be offered as surety for desire, and this is all the more true because the hysteric's primary aim is to paralyze the desire of the other. The more he loves his idealized object, the more protected he is from her desire. Hence he seeks to express a love without limit so as to conceal the other's lack. In this way, the hysteric presents himself as a hero sacrificed on the terrain of his love for the woman, as the one who can offer everything and thereby unconsciously make up for what he cannot give because he does not have it. This sacrificial dimension eventually turns him into a troubadour of courtly love, or, as the case may be, into a war veteran, mournful and unrecognized, with no pension to honor all the sacrifices made and services rendered in honor of the lady. He is therefore ready to prepare for the final battle in order to regain her.

This sacrifice usually has the opposite of the intended effect, since it confirms the woman's sense that her desire is being neutralized. In this confusion of desire and love, the hysteric is just paying the price for his inscription in the phallic function. The greater the expiatory debt, the more the hysteric's logic of desire finds a way to be dissatisfied. Indeed, the misunderstanding increases geometrically as love overtakes desire. As for the woman's desire, it decreases proportionately as the invasion of love blocks its living dynamic.

Although the erotic investment of a woman by the hysterical man can lead to behavior reminiscent of perversion, there is an absolute difference in the function served by the idealization or destruction of the woman, a difference caused by the respective phallic logics of hysterics and perverts. While for the pervert the woman is intended to challenge castration and keep it at bay, for the hysteric she is the most certain evidence of the solidity of his adhesion to castration.

To say that the pervert's disavowal basically refers to the mother's desire for the father is implicitly to acknowledge that what is being disavowed is sexual difference. And yet, as Freud so correctly observed, this denial can come about as such only because the pervert somehow does know about this desire on the mother's part. This is another way of saying that, even as he recognizes the real of sexual difference, the pervert is busy challenging its implications, of which the main one is considering sexual difference to be the signifying cause of desire. He therefore has to sustain the possibility of a *jouissance* that can do without this signifying cause. The only way to accomplish this, he believes, is to provoke and defy the law.

But, at the same time, it is through this constant provocation of the law that he assures and reassures himself that the law really does exist, that he can meet up with it and test out the economy of his *jouissance*. Thus transgression is the inevitable correlate of defiance. There is no better way to confirm the existence of the law than to try to transgress prohibitions and the laws that symbolically establish them. And the pervert always encounters the sanction he is looking for in this metonymic displacement of the transgression of prohibitions, since this sanction is the limit that refers, itself metonymically, to the limit of the prohibition of incest.

In short, the more the pervert defies and transgresses limits, the more he is seeking to assure himself that the law originates for everyone in sexual difference and the prohibition of incest. But this logic calls for vigilance regarding certain scenarios that may lead to diagnostic confusion with obsessional neurosis and hysteria.

In certain eventful moments of obsessional dynamics it is not unusual to find processes of transgression. In these cases, the transgression is directly connected to the obsessional's forward flight from his desire. Sometimes desire runs faster than the obsessional, who does not want to know anything about it: he is overtaken by the enactment of a desire that, most of the time, he experiences passively. He is thus in some sense kidnapped by his own desire, and it is in this context that the enactment is expressed as transgression.

Although this is usually an insignificant or pathetic transgression, it is always experienced by the subject as drama. Its occasionally spectacular nature makes it similar to a perverse transgression. Acting out is the way in which the obsessional gives himself permission to be acted on by his desire: he rushes headlong into the *jouissance* of transgression in spite of himself. But a crucial element is missing here, one that makes all the difference between this acting out and a genuine perverse transgression, namely defiance, at least in its special meaning in the realm of the perversions.

It is true that some defiant behaviors are clearly found among obsessionals. For example, obsessionals often compulsively engage in battles over control that are always based on the defiance of some adversity. Nevertheless, as soon as defiance enters into the obsessional strategy, the possibility of transgression disappears. In the atmosphere of "all-out mobilization" in which the obsessional is prepared to challenge adversity, he can do so only from the perspective of "regular combat." Any transgression becomes virtually impossible. Moreover, we know that it is precisely for this reason that he is so offended if the slightest rule is broken. And this is what suggests that, unconsciously, the obsessional tries desperately to be perverse but without ever succeeding. The more he becomes the defender of legality, the more he is struggling (often unwittingly) against his wish to transgress.

What the obsessional does not know, or want to know, about defiance is that he is usually the only protagonist. To undertake defiance, he has to create an imaginary situation of adversity, and this conceals the fact that he is almost always the one who is hurling challenges at himself. As a result, he needs a lot of noise, activity, and expenditure of energy to overcome them.

In hysteria, a different kind of diagnostic confusion has to be explained. Hysteria tends to be inclined toward transgression. The specific dynamics of the hysterical economy of desire often motivate the subject to perverse acting out. Underlying the transgression is a deep insecurity about identification stemming from the phallic stakes and their corollary, sexual identity.

The hysteric's fundamental ambiguity when it comes to his sexual identity often leads his desire in directions that recall the perverse profile. To mention only two characteristic examples, there is the perverse ambiguity expressed in the hysteric's homosexual acting out and the perverse *jouissance* of hysterics in getting at the truth, the position that Lacan describes as the "beautiful soul." Borrowed from Hegel, this term refers to the hysterical tendency to bring about the truth even if this means revealing before a third party the stakes of the desire of the other.

To remain with only these two examples, though there are others, we may observe that transgression in the context of hysteria is weakened by its typically perverse motivation. And, of course, this brings up the issue of defiance. Unlike that of the obsessional, the hysteric's defiance never questions the law of the father regarding the phallic logic and the signifier of castration. In hysteria, the signifier of castration is explicit, and it is the loss that is the price to be paid for the symbolization we find in the phallic demand. I have said that obsessionals are nostalgic for "being it," and hysterics could be called militants for "having it."

We have to be very careful about what is at stake in the hysteric's resort to defiance. Most often, the defiant element has to do with the dimension of seeming and not with the dimension of transgression as is the rule with the pervert. This aspect having to do with seeming is part of the strategy of phallic demand. A classic example is the hysterical woman's fantasmatic identification with the prostitute. It is always in a formidable phallic defiance that the hysteric walks the street or parks her car in a strategic place. But her *jouissance* in this defiance disappears as soon as she has the opportunity to retort to the incautious customer: "You're making a mistake. I'm not that kind of woman."

Another way in which the female hysteric shows defiance might be called "putting to the test" in disputing the phallus with a male partner. Here one of the favorite expressions is the classic taunt, "Without me, you'd be nothing!" This can be translated as, "I challenge you to prove to me that you really have what you supposedly have." As we know, the ill-advised partner has only to engage in such a demonstration for the hysteric to escalate the challenge.

In male hysteria, too, defiance also concerns the phallic attribution, but in another way. It is as though the male hysteric undertakes the strategy of defiance only when summoned by the desire of the female other. In this dialectic of desire he issues an untenable challenge *to himself*, untenable because it stems from an unconscious connection between desire and masculinity: being desired or desirable is understood only in terms of virility. Confused in this way, the male hysteric cannot desire a woman without proving his manhood. He gets caught up in this challenge, as pitiless as it is pitiful, of being unable to desire a woman unless he has the (fantasmatic) assurance that she will succumb if he shows this proof. In other words, the woman's *jouissance* is seen as the sign of capitulation to his phallic omnipotence. Trapped by this untenable and imaginary challenge, he usually has no other recourse but to respond in symptomatically familiar ways: premature ejaculation or impotence.

In the case of the female and the male hysteric alike, defiance has little in common with the perverse kind. As with the obsessional, defiance with regard to the possession of the phallic object is essentially situated in the alternative of having it or not having it. In the pervert, however, the problematics of defiance are quite different. Here what is being challenged is the law of the father. His defiance is thus essentially situated in the dialectic of being. We find this most strongly confirmed in the imperiousness with which he asserts the law of his desire. He tends to impose it as the sole law of desire that he recognizes, and not as the expression of a desire grounded in the law of the other's desire. Because this law of the desire of the other is originally the law of the father, we might say that the father dictates the law to the mother and the child. This law of the father, with everything it entails about a lack to be symbolized through castration, is what the pervert is permanently set on defying. In so doing, he defies the requirement that the law of his desire be subject to the law of the other's desire.

14

Perverse Jouissance *and the Complicit Third Party. Secrecy and Action*

Although the pervert is aware of the law, even if only to encounter it through defiance, the acting out of this provocation sometimes takes the most unexpected paths. Careful as they are to establish the foundations of all laws—beginning with the law of their own desire—perverts are inclined toward the transformation of the most basic values, whose originary legislation they attempt to ensure and extend. As Jean Clavreul (1985) observes, nowadays perverts are more integrated into society, and there is no so-called normal subject who is immune to the attraction of perversion.

It is in this sense that some perverts can become great moralists. Others prefer to exercise their talents in the mysteries of initiation, speculative reform, or education and even reeducation, thereby working to promote values they incessantly seek to fortify with regulations and laws. While some are skilled at exorcising the implacable logic of defiance and transgression that underlies these

spiritual endeavors, it is certainly not the case that the provoca-
tiveness of the pervert always finds expression in the service of
social values. Perhaps this is even what, for the pervert, separates
subversion from subornation. For the most part, the dividing line
between the two seems to depend on the fate of perverse *jouissance*
and the ease with which it can be sublimated.

The pervert is usually not eager to pursue this *jouissance* unless he has a chance to lead astray the ally who can help him de-
ploy it: the complicit third party who acts as mediator.

The pervert's *jouissance* seems to be located in a middle ground
in which he pretends to feel the psychic stakes that constitute his
backbone: on the one hand, the primacy of the law of his desire as
the only possible law of desire, and, on the other hand, the recognition of the desire of the other as the mediating factor in everyone's
desire. With regard to these two options, perverse *jouissance* uti-
lizes an impossible strategy of conciliation. This strategy is designed
both to evoke in a third party the conviction that this *jouissance*
may perhaps not be perverse and, at the same time, to entrap him
in it. Thus the pervert first posits the law of the father (and castration) as an existing limit, so as to go on to show that it is perhaps
not a fixed law since one can always take the risk of overstepping
it. This strategy of overstepping is where the pervert finds his
jouissance. But the strategist's pleasure cannot be obtained without the complicity—imaginary or real—of a third party who wit-
nesses, dumbfounded, the pervert's fantasmatic conjuring trick
with regard to castration.

The summoning of this third party, necessary to sustain perverse *jouissance*, is always the metonymic reiteration of the original third who bore him and sustained him, namely the mother. In
a brilliant study of the perversions, Jean Clavreul (1967) explains
why the gaze of the third is required:

It is clear that it is as bearer of the gaze that the Other will be the partner, above all the accomplice, in the perverse act. Here we are dealing with the radical distinction between perverse practice, where the gaze of the Other is an indispensable part of the complicity without which the illusion would not exist, and perverse fantasy, which not only can do quite well without the gaze of the Other but must find its outcome in solitary masturbation. If the perverse act is clearly distinct from the enacted fantasy, it is the gaze of the Other that is the boundary line, a gaze whose complicity is needed by the pervert whereas it is condemnatory for the normal or the neurotic. [pp. 108–109]

The perverse strategy is exceptionally fixed, even if its acting out is as excited as we know it to be. As Clavreul notes, the strategy involves corrupting the other in terms of his orientation points and limits within the law: "What is most important for the pervert is that the Other be sufficiently engaged, sufficiently inscribed in familiar orientation points especially of respectability, that each new experience will seem to be a debauch, that is, that the Other will be taken out of his system and will agree to a *jouissance* of which the pervert has confident control" (pp. 109–110).

As we might expect, in the actions he takes to extend his *jouissance* the pervert resorts to his favorite techniques, defiance and transgression. One of the primary elements in this regard is secrecy, which by its nature is a magnet for transgression. Before we examine the basis of this strategy as it is enacted, a look at obsessional neurosis will clarify what is distinctive about the transgression of secrecy in the case of the pervert.

There is no everyday situation in life that does not preoccupy the obsessional, at least to some degree, with the question of secrecy. Most often, this entails his being imprisoned in it. What is so pathetic about this imprisonment is that the obsessional's secret is an open one. While it is obvious to the careful observer, the obsessional is under the illusion that he alone shares it. This strategy of keeping secret something that he unwittingly reveals all the time has to do with the structuring mechanisms of undoing and isolation.

As a rule, the secret involves the revelation of the desire that the subject is desperately trying to ward off through displacement. When he has completely worn himself out trying to maintain this distance, his last symptomatic defense is to turn it into a secret. He cherishes this secret, savors it, loves it in silence. And the more he ruminates on it, the more secret it seems to him. As he harps on it endlessly and laboriously, his *jouissance* is kept going by a persistent fantasy: the surprising effect he will have on the day he reveals the secret. This anticipation involves a host of fantasmatic circumstances in which the obsessional's essential sadism is to be found. This is why he cannot imagine the disclosure of the secret as anything other than an explosion, a revolution beyond repair that will annihilate the other with its unexpected violence. In this imaginary scenario, his *jouissance* increases in direct proportion to the expansion of his strategic rumination.

When the obsessional is finally ready to reveal his secret, he prepares adroitly. He subtly refines his plan of attack and, in a surge of heroism, proceeds to confession. But, contrary to his every expectation, when the truth comes to light it is nothing more than a sorry balloon that has burst. His warlike strategy amounts to beating a dead horse. No one was fooled except the strategist himself, who is distressed to see that all he has produced are a few splashes when he thought he would bring on a tidal wave.

This wholly typical obsessional strategy is different in every detail from the pervert's manipulation of secrecy. The pervert is well aware of what is really at stake in a secret. In contrast to the obsessional, he is able to distinguish between an open secret and a true one marked by a prohibition of saying and doing. A genuine secret has the advantage of being continually defied. Strengthened by his ability to challenge the law, that is, prohibition, the pervert sets about to prove that a secret can always be revealed.

In order for the pervert to obtain the highest degree of *jouissance* as a result of his efforts, the revelation must take place under certain conditions. What must happen is that the pervert indicate that secrecy can be transgressed indirectly, without his having had anything to do with it. Hence the need for a third party, whose timely mediation consists in letting himself be trapped in an unspoken collusion against someone else.

Secrecy presupposed at least two protagonists: one who knows and another who does not, implicitly connected with one another in a bond of dependence. For there to be real secrecy, one of these protagonists must know that the other possesses something that cannot be mentioned. In the initial phase, the perverse strategy involves making sure that one party believes the other to know something about him secretly. He is exceptionally skillful in the arts of allusion and rhetorical subornation that will arouse suspicion. Having achieved his ends, all he has to do is manipulate matters so that he can transgress secrecy by proxy.

But if this proxy action requires the presence of a third party, the latter must be "conditioned" regarding the secret and its revelation. He must be caught up in a complicit set of alternatives. On the one hand, his envy must be aroused by giving him to understand that there is someone else who would very much like to know the secret that the pervert is keeping. On the other hand, he must also be given to understand that the revelation of the secret would be detrimental to that person: hence the need for silence.

It is obviously this injunction to silence that piques the curiosity of the third party and traps him in the complicity of a secret that is supposedly in the other's interest. At most it is enough to insist adroitly on the necessity and benefit of silence for the third party to be hopelessly caught up in the perverse strategy. In this Machiavellian process, an atmosphere of confidence is created with the third party so that, at the right moment, the secret can be revealed, the point being to make its contents known along with a garnish of ethical prescriptions designed to oblige the third party to confidentiality. When this crucial moment has been reached, the perverse strategy has been accomplished. The pervert can then reap the awaited harvest of *jouissance*.

The third party finds himself a captive in the complicit possession of a secret without noticing that what seals the bond of complicity is not confidence but guilt. The pervert, having managed to make the third party guilty of knowing a secret that could harm another, knows that this is what will lead to transgression. The third party must either keep silent and feel guilty about it or reveal the secret and feel just as guilty for having been the agent of a misfortune that the pervert had warned him about. A prisoner, suffering because he possesses something he cannot speak about, he identifies with the other, whom he imagines to be likewise suffering because he is deprived of a truth about himself. He therefore ends up confessing the secret to him. But he cannot make this confession except by presenting this truth as something he himself was not supposed to know. And the revelation imposes silence on the other, since now he too has been let into the confidence of the secret. The other possesses a truth about himself that he must keep silent about in order not to harm his benefactor, the third party, whom he would betray to the pervert if he made the revelation known. Guilt has been shifted around; it is now the interested party who is trapped by a truth he can say no more about.

By this point, the pervert's *jouissance* is completely guaranteed, not only because of the transitivity of speech but because of the transitivity associated with secrecy itself. He knows that the other knows and has the assurance that the other also knows that he must act as if he did not. The pervert's greatest delight will then be to set up a meeting with the other so as to savor the transgressing of the prohibition, accomplished in such a way that none of the protagonists can confess. It is as though there were no interdiction, no transgression, since in this meeting everything is implicitly known in such a way that nothing can be communicated about the way in which the secret was found out.

There are several situations that are especially favorable to this perverse enactment. To give only one example, I will describe the misfortune that befell an analyst who was the victim of a perverse Machiavellian intrigue.[1]

One day during his office hours, this analyst received an initial visit from a man of about 40, who quickly turned out to be a formidable pervert. The treatment got underway with difficulty, and several times a week the analyst had to sit through a personal recital of his patient's thousand and one depravities. The patient led a totally dissolute life devoted to perverse eccentricities of the most disturbing and scandalous kind.

After some time, the analyst, a highly experienced man of a certain age, was able to identify several intriguing themes. Since perverts are usually very sensitive to the art of manipulation, this patient, sure that he was arousing a great deal of curiosity in his analyst, had begun to give more and more details about his life. For several months he described past and current illegal activities, lies, and scandals, situations in which the protagonists could not talk about what was happening. His was an absolutely frenetic existence of criminal debauchery in which sexual oddity seemed to know no limit.

---

1. This material was presented in the strictest confidence during a study group on the perversions that I organized in another country.

The analyst thus became the auditory witness to the most disturbing transgressions involving theft, swindling, illegal trafficking, and rape that sometimes made headlines. It is clear that this necessarily secret complicity brought the patient enormous *jouissance* in the very place where he was supposed to be receiving treatment, this *jouissance* being all the greater because it was guaranteed by the analyst's silence. Several episodes of acting out even managed to make the analyst a juridical accomplice to illegal situations he was unavoidably privy to.

Nevertheless, the treatment continued because of the olympian firmness of the analyst, constantly put to the test. Precisely because the analyst remained immovable, the patient resorted to his final strategy. Now, it is often the case in perversion that the last strategy is the decisive one, in that it never gives away its purpose, the point of the perverse maneuver being to adjust the target for as long as it takes to be able to score a bull's eye. The course of the analysis soon took a new turn. With each session the patient became more and more voluble about his perverse love affairs, providing minute sexual details to the point where the analytic hours almost became unbearable. These scenes often involved the same protagonists, giving themselves over to acrobatic excesses that could scarcely be imagined and that were, to say the least, very dangerous. It was as though there was a constant challenge to that irreversible limit known as death.

The analyst eventually came to believe that his patient was becoming greatly disturbed and would be in danger if there were no stop to this excess of *jouissance*. This phase of getting carried away with *jouissance*, which represents a kind of plea addressed by the patient to the analyst, is common in the treatment of perverts and is to be understood as a sign of impending rupture. In the best-case scenario, it is the patient who abruptly breaks off treatment. But it may happen that the break occurs because of tragic acting out on the patient's part.

In this treatment, it was as though the analyst felt himself becoming more and more personally involved in the torrent of unbearable reports regularly brought in by his patient. Overcome by increasing anxiety, the analyst, unaware of what he was doing, slipped from the place he had maintained up to this point and became more directive. This was a fatal slippage if there ever was one, since this was the signal the patient had been waiting for in order to make the final attack in his perverse project. He began to seem more and more horrifying to the analyst as he subtly revealed the identity of his protagonists: there gradually emerged a group of eminent personages, including some from the best intellectual circles.

A full year and a half of treatment was necessary in order for this patient to accomplish his destructive mission and disappear immediately afterwards. He had no concern for the consequences of taking defiance and transgression to their most dire extremes. Considering the analyst ripe for a final revelation, he revealed the identity of one of his most depraved and lewd sexual partners: she was none other than one of the analyst's daughters.

Part III

On the Borders of the Perversions

15

Structural Proximity of the Psychoses and the Perversions

The establishment of the perverse process, as we have seen, is directly dependent on the signifying messages through which the mother and father transmit something of the nature of their mutual desire. This does not mean that the subject is the helpless victim of these conjoined desires; the child is not an innocent being, prey to the logical implications of the desire of the other. He is a protagonist in his own right, since he is himself a creature of desire, a desiring creature. From this perspective, his position is one of totalitarian power, in that he is the agent of a considerable inertial force of desire.

Indeed, there is something dictatorial about the child's desire that must interfere in the Other's dynamics of desire. This desiring inertia that carries the child toward and against everything, leading him to offer himself as an object that will fill the lack in the Other (the phallus), can have a considerable effect on the phallic harmony of the family circle. To mention only one example, consider the eruption of psychotic processes in only one child of a set of siblings. This shows the degree to which the child's desiring inertia can, at certain moments, call forth the desiring synergy of the parents in a disastrous way.

The phallic function is inscribed in a quadratic structure: the mother, the father, the child, and the phallus. The combination of these elements can lead to different interactions. But we can define the logic of these interactions only if we understand the meaning of the first three terms, among themselves, in relation to the fourth, the phallic element that is the signifier of castration and the law. If we keep this in mind, we can define a number of characteristic structural implications, some of which have the potential for interacting among themselves as border phenomena. This is the meaning of the signifier of the law, enabling us to understand both the proximity of these structural organizations and the dividing line that separates them and gives them a radical autonomy. This seems to be the case with the psychoses and the perversions, which certainly explains the clinical frequency of perverse manifestations in certain psychotics.

To say that the signifier of the law is the decisive factor in the establishment of perverse and psychotic processes is to emphasize the major importance of the place from which this signifier will signify for the subject. For there is a difference between the signifier of the law and the signifying of the law. We might even say that it is this difference that allows the pervert to escape psychosis. The distinction is maintained for the pervert, if only in a very marginal way. The signifier of the law continues to refer to the sole agency that can guarantee its operative power: the paternal agency. The pervert's attribution of the phallus to the mother is possible only under this condition. Although he is aware that she has no penis, it is still the case that he registers this lack only with reference to the one who does have it. The paternal phallic attribution thus appears on the horizon of the pervert's fantasmatic interrogation of sexual difference. Even in this limiting sense it thus remains present, though it coexists with the contradictory attribution of the phallus to the mother.

In the psychotic, on the other hand, the confusion between the signifier of the law and the phallic signifier is complete. This is why the child's phallic identification continues to predominate. Signifying never occurs only because a signifier is associated with a signified. In itself, the signifier does not produce meaning. It is a mere acoustic image, as Saussure put it. But the fundamentally structuring nature of the metaphor of the Name-of-the-Father has to do with the fact that this symbolic operation produces signification. The signifier Name-of-the-Father is effective only because it does not remain a pure signifier; it is associated with the signified of the mother's desire (if only metaphorically). This operation makes all the difference between the symbolization of the law and the foreclosing of the signifier Name-of-the-Father.

The foreclosing of the Name-of-the-Father (for details, see Dor 1985, Ch. 13 and 14) occurs when this signifier cannot enter into a process of signifying, that is, cannot join with a signified so as to symbolize the paternal phallic attribution. Nevertheless, if we are to agree with Lacan (1957b) that the foreclosure of the Name-of-the-Father is "the defect that gives psychosis its essential condition and the structure that separates it from neurosis" (p. 215), certain clarifications are needed. In particular, we have to explain the relation between foreclosure and the problem of castration. It is not enough to state, as Lacan does, that the signifier Name-of-the-Father never reached the symbolic level. For we might understand this to mean that, with the foreclosure of the Name-of-the-Father, the symbolic itself never arrived as such: it is as though this paternal reference made it exist for the subject.

This critical hypothesis formulated by Alain Juranville (1984) presupposes that, if the symbol did not exist for the subject, he would lack all knowledge. But how, then, are we to understand that the subject avoids or rejects something (*Verwerfung*) of which he has no knowledge?

Clearly, the Name-of-the-Father is foreclosed because of what it evokes or signifies. Thus we must hold that the psychotic has a certain experience of castration, even if it has no symbolic insertion in the sense that he does not symbolize it. Lacan does make this point in his seminar on the psychoses (1955–1956, p. 12). Thus foreclosure has to do with something that, in some way, has already taken on the meaning of castration. But some additional clarification is called for so that Lacan's hypothesis about the triggering of the psychoses will not be too enigmatic. In his paper entitled "On a Question Preliminary to Any Possible Treatment of Psychosis" (1957b), Lacan explains that "the Name-of-the-Father, *verworfen*, foreclosed, that is to say, never having attained the place of the Other, must be called in to symbolic opposition to the subject" (p. 217). It is mainly in connection with the phrase "never having attained the place of the Other" that there might be some contradiction with Lacan's account of foreclosure. This "never having attained" does not seem to entail a radical absence of a signifying paternal reference. If it did, we would once again be faced with the objection noted above. The foreclosure of the Name-of-the-Father can be considered a rejection of castration only if we presume a certain knowledge of castration in the psychotic. But—and this is the important point—the psychotic refuses to be subject to this knowledge. Speaking of the Wolf Man, Lacan (1955–1956) calls attention to "the fact that he has rejected all means of access to castration, which is nevertheless apparent in his conduct, all access to the register of the symbolic function, *the fact that any assumption of castration by an I has become impossible for him*" (p. 13, emphasis added).

This is why the foreclosure of the Name-of-the-Father unambiguously refers to the "I don't want to know anything about it" that enables the psychotic to maintain his imaginary identification with the phallus by denying the existence of lack. Here, as Juranville (1984, p. 276) so aptly puts it, the knowledge of castration persists, as does the knowledge of the Other, but the psychotic does not want to be its subject. As a result, the Other is eliminated from the circuit of speech, in such a way that true speech on the part of a subject is excluded.

With regard to the signifier Name-of-the-Father, it thus becomes possible to make an essential distinction between the perversions and the psychoses. In the perversions, the structure involves the process of symbolization of the law. The element Name-of-the-Father has taken its place as a substitute for the signifier of the mother's desire. Foreclosure is avoided in favor of primal repression. Nevertheless, the phallic signifier lends itself to this metaphoric substitution only on certain conditions, especially that of the "short circuit" that intervenes on the level of the attribution of this signifier. Although, in the perversions, the phallic signifier serves as a referent in the place of a paternal attribution, it is still the case that this attribution remains a supposition, given that the father has not been able to offer proof of it. This lack of proof leads to a "short circuit" that gives the phallic signifier an ambiguous reference. It pertains to the father in the mother's discourse, but it returns to the maternal agency that, as we have seen, becomes the potential depositary of the phallic attribution delegated to her by paternal complicity.

This "short circuit" in the locating of the phallic signifier mobilizes a specific process of internal functioning. It is no longer a case of foreclosure, as for the psychotic, but of the disavowal of castration. Moreover, given the absence of a stable inscription on the level of the paternal reference, the signifier will remain in a symbolic middle ground, thereby producing one of the most characteristic effects of perverse functioning, namely the rush into a contradictory dynamic with regard to castration. The pervert is continually projected toward a "beyond" of castration that he always ends up discovering to be a place on this side of it. It is precisely on the "this side" of castration that the psychotic is estranged in the imprisonment of phallic identification.

In this connection, we must go on to develop a fuller account of another distinction that we have already touched on: the difference between the phallic mother and the mother outside the law. In no way can the phallic mother be considered the mother outside the law as Lacan describes her. The phallic mother embodies the law for the child in that she is its ambassador. She "represents" it herself to the precise degree that there has been a transfer to her of the symbolic locus from which the reference to the law is signified. As a symbolic function, the paternal function does indeed exist, except that, having been delegated to the mother, it exists as something of an ambiguity for the pervert. Mediated by the maternal agency, the law is marked by a certain denaturation in its symbolic resonance. For the pervert, the law is inscribed not as a law that subjects one's desire to the law of the desire of the other, but as an unjust law that commands the pervert to transgress it in order to try to sustain it in his own fashion.

To say, "There is no law," in other words, to imagine that the mother (or the woman) necessarily has a phallus, is already to transgress the law. This enables us to understand perverse *jouissance*. To make law is in effect to command *jouissance* in advance. The law the pervert obeys is the law of *jouissance*, as Lacan explains it in his magisterial study, "Kant avec Sade" (1962, pp. 765–790).

But, as Lacan observes, although the Other exists, the pervert never refers to the Other except in his will to *jouissance*. This is another way of saying that he "makes himself the instrument of the Other's *jouissance*" (Lacan 1960, p. 320) by offering himself as the very locus of the accomplishment of transgression. The original aim of this transgression is to embody the phallic signifier in reality by trying to divert the essential scope of the signification of castration. For this signification, by its nature, "disembodies" any possibility of objectivation of the phallic signifier and, conversely, requires that the phallus never be inscribed in reality except as the signifier of lack. The clearest illustration of the pervert's resistance to the absence of any real objectivation of the phallus is his investment of the fetish object that is substituted for the phallus and the lack it presupposes.

As Piera Aulagnier (1964) notes in a remarkable study, to the same extent that the phallic mother has understood the meaning of the law so as to represent it herself, the mother outside the law seems to have understood nothing whatsoever of this signification, since she has usually been unable to symbolize it for herself. This is why the mother of the future psychotic represents the law in the child's eyes. Such a law is an entirely personal one that in no way refers to the phallic signifier and castration. And Aulagnier rightly emphasizes the individual nature of this law. The child can only remain subjected to maternal omnipotence.

As for the pervert, he invests the mother as omnipotent insofar as he diligently elaborates the fantasy of her phallic attribution. But in the context of the psychoses, it is the mother who invests herself as omnipotent for the child; there is no omnipotence that is referred in one way or another to the paternal agency. When the paternal function has been completely denied by the mother where the child is concerned, the phallic signifier supported by the Name-of-the-Father is foreclosed. As a result, the child is neither recognized nor designated by the mother's discourse as inscribed in a lineage. The child is never invested and signified as daughter or son of a father. The mother of the future psychotic does not submit her desire to the law of the other's desire and thereby disavows the paternal reference, the reference to castration. A captive, forced to identify with the mother's imaginary phallus, the child is condemned to an unending quest for an answer to the question of maternal desire. Only the signifier Name-of-the-Father, by offering the sole answer to this enigma, opens up the space of a knowledge, access to which is forbidden. Such a knowledge is the only limit that can put an end to the unceasing quest concerning the mother's desire. The absence of this limit opens up a universe of void, within which the child destructively exhausts himself trying to fulfill a maternal desire whose signification is not halted by anything coming to the child's rescue.

This is the fundamental reason why perverse and psychotic structures are so close and, at the same time, so dissimilar: the space between them is one of crucial symbolic mediation.

Because of this closeness that is essentially connected to the interaction of the phallic signifier in the logic of the paternal function, certain trajectories of escape become possible. In these trajectories of escape, the destiny of the phallic signifier seems to be obliged to recognize a unique limiting outcome. This outcome is put to the test in the most radical way in the transsexual saga. In transsexualism, the phallic signifier is in fact abolished from the imaginary register, but without thereby becoming inscribed in that of the symbolic. The phallic identification snatched away from the imaginary seems to get bogged down in the real, unable to attain the only status that is its own: the symbolic status of sexual difference. From this point of view, as we shall see, for the transsexual the phallic signifier is assigned an asymptotic fate, since it is offered to the unending task of supporting an impossible sexual identity by attempting to identify with the signifier of sexual difference itself. If such a sexual identity turns out to be impossible, it is so only with regard to the vicissitudes of the phallic attribution that govern the ordinary course of sexual identity in accordance with the requirements prescribed by sexuation.

16

Sexuation, Sexual Identity, and Vicissitudes of Phallic Attribution

To recognize that the child is led into the play of identifications as a result of the paternal metaphor is to become aware that the possibility of situating oneself as a man or a woman is directly connected to the symbolization of the law and of castration. The problematics of sexual identity are thus totally dependent on the relation each of us maintains with the phallic attribution.

Thus the absence of the signifier Name-of-the-Father will inevitably give rise to disturbances of sexual identity. For proof of this, we have only to consider the canonical example of the torment suffered by President Schreber with regard to his virility, alternately expressed in hallucinations of evisceration and emasculation. His radical identification with the phallus led him to the delusion of becoming a woman in the sense that Lacan points out when he observes that "it is not by being foreclosed from the penis, but by having to be the phallus that the patient is doomed to become a woman" (1957b, p. 207, translation modified). And Lacan continues: "No doubt the divination of the unconscious very soon warned the subject that, incapable as he is of being the phallus that the mother lacks, he is left with the solution of being the phallus that men lack" (p. 207).

With the psychotic's imaginary delusion of feminization, we are at the borderland of transsexualism, which seems to be a pathological intermediary position halfway between the psychoses and the perversions. To understand this middle ground, we must take a closer look at the question of sexual identity beyond the Freudian corpus itself, that is, through Lacan's further theorizations and explanatory commentaries on sexuation. These studies, confirmed by everyday clinical experience, lead us to realize that, if the assumption of our sexual identity as speaking subjects is fundamentally dependent on the phallic function, we have to accept the secondary nature of the anatomical specification of the sexes in our assurance of being a woman or a man. But an assurance is not a certainty, the only certainty we never have being precisely that of the anatomical specification of our sex.

From the perspective of our sexual identity, we cannot speak of certainty but at most of a feeling of sexual belonging to a feminine or masculine gender. This suggests that we must distinguish two levels in the problematics of sexual identity. The first is the real of our sexual anatomy, the second our sexual identity itself, which results from a psychic elaboration on the basis of the real. The inevitable mediation of such a psychic process may destine the sexual identity of the speaking subject to a number of vicissitudes. Yet defining them as different possibilities must not make us lose sight of the fact that these avenues of realization are programmed by the subject's relation to the phallus.

What is this relation? It is above all a relation to the real of sexual difference, the real that brings about the phallic object itself. Sexual identity is won at the end of a voyage that originates in an imaginary cartography, and this is why there is a possible discrepancy between the anatomical sexuation and the sexual identity of the subject. To place the phallic object at the epicenter of the process of sexual identity is to emphasize the question of the phallic attribution and the dynamics of the circulation of the phallus. Without these two landmarks, it would be very difficult to say with any precision what is at stake in the highly unusual sexual identity of transsexuals. On the other hand, however, saying what is so eccentric about the transsexual's attempt at identity presupposes that we have a clear notion of the principle governing the sexual bipartition of speaking subjects with regard to the phallic function. Lacan's studies of the process of sexuation[1] are extremely helpful in explaining the structural impossibility of transsexual identity. We shall also have to examine the fluctuations of sexual identity in the context of phallic attribution.

THE PROCESS OF SEXUATION ACCORDING TO LACAN[2]

If our sexual identity as speaking subjects is dependent on the effects of the unconscious, this implies that anatomical sex is never the most certain indication of that identity. This ambiguity is clarified by Lacan's formulas of sexuation:

---

1. The development of Lacan's theories on the problematics of sexuation takes place in the course of a number of works: 1969–1970; 1970–1971; 1971–1972 a and b; 1972, which is a magisterial but difficult study, summing up in a condensed and allusive way most of the formulations up to this time; and the clearer exposition in 1972–1973.

2. This summary of the problematics of sexuation was presented at a seminar in Buenos Aires on October 30, 1986 at the invitation of the psychoanalyst Teresa Zavalia.

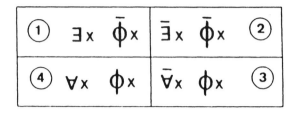

The logical formulas in this table represent the four scenarios of the phallic function. But these formulas are meaningful only if understood two by two, since they reflect the bipartition of speaking subjects from the point of view of their sexual identity as men and women. Men's sexual identity is represented by formulas 1 and 4, women's by 2 and 3. All speaking subjects line up on one or the other side according to their mode of inscription in the phallic function.

Since the sexual identity of men and women depends on the phallic object, we might automatically suppose that the distribution of the sexes is made on the basis of having or not having the phallus. If that were the case, we would need only two scenarios and two logical formulas. On the one hand, we would have the affirmative universal proposition $\forall x\, \Phi x$: for every x, the property Φ applies. In other words, "All men fulfill the phallic function" or "All men have the phallus." On the other hand, we would have the negative universal proposition $\forall x\, \overline{\Phi}x$: for every x, the property Φ applies to no x. In other words, "No woman has the phallus."

This reductive logical notation is impossible. It is based on a fantasy that is utterly inconsistent due to castration and the Symbolic Father. This is why Lacan not only introduces other logical formulas but suggests notational modifications so as to take the phallic function into account. Formulas 2 and 3 are illegitimate in contemporary mathematical symbolic logic, but the modifications represent what Lacan calls the authentic knowledge of the psychoanalyst (1971–1972a). It is this authentic knowledge that leads him to propose two formulas that are as legitimate as they are provocative: "There is no sexual relation" and "Woman does not exist."

These two spectacular propositions explain the logical entailments of the bipartition of sexual identities. Let us return to the table presenting the four formulas. As I have noted, these must be understood in groups of two in order to account for sexual difference.

At this point, a brief detour to the question of the equality of the sexes is in order, if only to expose the crude imaginary deception that underlies this idea. It is radically impossible to think of the sexes as equal, since all that exists is difference. On the other hand, we can legitimately speak of a legality of the sexes. And it is because there is difference that such legality is not only conceivable but mandatory. Conversely, it is precisely this legality of the sexes that precludes the existence of any equality. What is more, it means that the sexuation of women can be understood only on the basis of the sexuation of men. This is in no way a phallocratic position but a simple consequence of phallic logic. Only the sexual identity of men can institute a legality of the sexes and do so, moreover, by founding the universality of this legal difference.

Let us consider some everyday expressions. For example, "Let's talk man to man" or "We spoke as equals." These are typically masculine expressions that have no equivalent in the discourse of women. Women do not say " as equals" or "woman to woman"; what they say is "between women." Is this a coincidence? Not at all. The solidarity in masculine equality can be explained only in terms of the phallic function, which creates the possibility of an egalitarian male *jouissance*. Things are different for women.

What makes a man feel that he is legally entitled to be the equal of another man? It is phallic logic, whereby every man is obliged to exist in the framework of a certain universality. Women, on the other hand, are—as Lacan puts it—*not all* inscribed in this universality.

Let us analyze the four formulas in the above table. Men's sexual identity is represented by formulas 1 and 4. Formula 4, the affirmative universal proposition $\forall x\, \Phi x$, indicates that all men are subject to the phallic function, that is, to castration. This follows from the existence of the symbolic father, the one who is said by Freud in "Totem and Taboo" (1912–1913) to be the father of the primal horde who possesses all the women. As such, he was the man who was not subject to castration, since the prohibition of incest had not been established. According to Freud's myth, it was because this despot possessed all the women that the sons rebelled, killed him, and ate him in a cannibalistic feast. Seized with remorse, they then promulgated the law of the prohibition of incest that not only set up the tyrant in the place of the symbolic father (that is, the dead father) but at the same time instituted the filiation of children from the father's side. In thus paying symbolic homage to the father, they made castration the correlative of the law.

In this sense, if all men are subject to castration ($\forall x\, \Phi x$), this is because there was at least one man who was exempt from it: the symbolic father of the primal horde in Freud's myth.

The affirmative universal proposition ($\forall x\, \Phi x$) is therefore based on the negative particular proposition $\exists x\, \bar{\Phi} x$, which means: there is at least one man who does not obey the phallic function, because he is exempt from castration. It is this x, not subject to the phallic function, that makes it necessary for all others to face castration. Here we have the primary value of the phallic function as support of the law.

Some conclusions are obvious at this point. For one thing, we can speak of a universality where men are concerned. They constitute a set, the universal set of all those who, without exception, are subject to castration. Because there is such a universal set, we may legitimately use a general term like "man." Moreover, the existence of the man who is exempt from the phallic function, namely the symbolic father, establishes the fantasy of an absolute *jouissance*, not subject to castration. But this *jouissance* of one single male entails for all others a *jouissance* that is inaccessible and forbidden.

These are the phallic prescriptions that determine the man's sexuation, that is, his sexual identity. Let us now turn to formulas 2 and 3, which express the mode of inscription of women in the phallic function. One feature is very conspicuous: neither of them expresses universality:

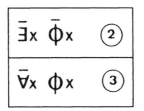

This indicates that woman are *not-all* subject to the phallic function, hence not entirely subject to castration and the law. In fact, in formula 3, the negation refers to the symbol $\forall$ ("for any . . . whatsoever"), which means: "It is not the case for every x that x obeys the phallic function."

And there is another special feature of formula 2. This formula indicates that there is no x that is not an exception to the phallic function, to castration. We cannot write, as we can for men, "There is at least one who is exempt from the phallic function ($\exists x\ \Phi x$). The "at least one" feminine subject escaping castration is missing. Nevertheless, we must understand formula 2 in connection with formula 3. Formula 3 does not mean that women have no relation to the phallic function, but simply that, for women, the phallic function is not limited, as it is for men, by the exception of one subject who is free of castration.

Several important conclusions can be drawn from this special feature. For women, nothing sets a limit to their *jouissance* by being a *jouissance* that is absolute and forbidden. Thus the prohibition of incest is not logically inscribed in the same way for women and for men. And the absence of this "at least one" woman who is exempt from castration makes any universalization impossible. Contrary to men, women do not constitute a universal set with regard to the phallic function. Logically there is no general legitimate expression to designate women. A universal expression like "Woman" is thus inadmissible. Hence Lacan's conclusion: "W̶o̶m̶a̶n̶ does not exist." He inscribes this impossibility by writing a bar. Woman exists *not-all*—not entirely—as a universal, and this is indicated in formula 3.

But while women are not-all subject to the phallic function, this in no way means that they are not at all subject to it. It simply emphasizes the fact that we can find no x that is an exception to this function. Thus women have not universality but contingency, a contingency (not all) that presupposes the impossible (since no x escapes function Φ).

Women's relation to *jouissance* is necessarily different from that of men. As Lacan puts it, theirs is an "other" relation to *jouissance*, since, unlike men, they do not have an absolute *jouissance* that is at the same time inaccessible and forbidden. For men, phallic *jouissance* is always a relation to the *jouissance* of the Other, which is forbidden. But women's *jouissance* has a different relation to the *jouissance* of the Other. As for men, the *jouissance* of the Other is impossible for them, but this impossibility does not represent a prohibition. Hence the possibility of a supplementary *jouissance* is open to women. It is what Lacan calls the "surplus *jouissance*" in designating women's special relation to the *jouissance* of the Other.

The expression "Woman does not exist" conveys something of this special relation to phallic *jouissance*. For Woman to exist, we would have to presume the myth of "at least one woman" (like "one" Symbolic Father), who would represent for all women a site of *jouissance* equivalent to that of the father of the primal horde: an impossible and forbidden *jouissance* that would entail an escape from castration. We would thus have, as for men, a limit for all other women with regard to the phallic function. A universality would be possible. This Woman would be equivalent to the Name-of-the-Father. And yet this signifier, Name-of-the-Father, being the phallic signifier, is necessarily unique.

It follows that, if Woman does not exist, there is no sexual relation. For there to be a relation to sex between a man and a woman, the man, as an element of a universality, would have to enter into relation with the woman, herself an element of a universality. Only on this condition could a relation be established in the logical sense. In logic, a relation is necessarily a mode of attribution. If such an attribution were logically possible, we could write the following relations: "The man is the woman's x" and "The woman is the man's x." But since the woman is not-all, "there is no sexual relation." Because the phallic *jouissance* of men and women is necessarily different, their encounter in the sex act always produces a lack that is the clearest proof of the imaginary nature of the sexual relation and of the complementarity of the *jouissances*. This lack, however, is a permanent invitation to the repetition of the sex act, the imaginary aim of which is always the possibility of an authentic relation of the *jouissances*.

It is thus futile to imagine an equality of the sexes. Even if some people bemoan that fact and actually demand such an equality, there is simply a radical difference between the *all* and the *not-*

all. On the other hand, this difference is what makes it possible for us to experience *jouissance* in the sex act and to repeat this *jouissance* as often as we wish. So every cloud has a silver lining!

SEXUAL IDENTITY AND THE VICISSITUDES OF PHALLIC ATTRIBUTION

We must be clear about the meaning of the expression *phallic attribution*. First of all, phallic attribution has no meaning apart from the mysteries of the Oedipus, an imaginary dialectic if there ever was one, in which the child tries to symbolize sexual difference. All the twists and turns of the Oedipus inevitably come together at the point where the phallic attribution becomes necessary, where the subject must come under the yoke of *having*. The metaphor of coming under the yoke is a fitting one, since, according to Lacan, a step must be taken that, in retrospect, brings the subject to a point of no return in the conquest of sexual identity. Lacan reminds us of how crucial this moment is: "In order to have it, the question must first have arisen of not having it; the possibility of being castrated is essential in the assumption of the fact of having the phallus. This is the step that must be taken. This is where, at some moment, the father must effectively, really, truly intervene" (1957–1958, seminar of January 1, 1958).

Note the emphasis placed here on the fact that, when it comes to the phallic attribution, the father is *not without having it* on the strict condition that he be able to prove what is attributed to him. This is the only condition under which the child is able to symbolize castration. He is then able to move on to the processes of identification that are subject to the dimension of having, and in this way feminine or masculine sexual identity is won, commensurate with the phallic attribution and castration.

A similar bipolarization of sexual identity governs the heterosexual exchange in a logic appropriate to the dynamics of desire. For, although a woman presumes that he has the phallic attribution, a man is not less castrated than she is. He does not have it, since he too had to renounce it. In heterosexual intercourse, the man gives the woman only what he does not have. But in offering this gift of what he does not have, he saves the woman from confusing the penis with the object of this act of gift-giving, which is the phallus. This ensures the ongoing role of intercourse in maintaining lack and the keenness of desire. From this point of view, the dialectic of heterosexual intercourse is one of the phallic gift.

In this way, the possibility of the circulation of the phallus attests to feminine and masculine sexual identity. But this kind of reciprocal possibility of sexual identity depends on a twofold condition: first, the phallic attribution that the father was able to demonstrate, and, second, the castration that results for the person who is confronted with that proof. As François Perrier and Wladimir Granoff (1979) rightly note in their study of female perversion, "the man cannot give what he has not lost, and can only lose what he has not renounced because he did not pay the debt of castration" (p. 83).

Potentialities for sexual identity other than the feminine and masculine identities that find their mutual confirmation in heterosexuality can come to be organized around these dialectical stakes. Insofar as sexual identity emerges, in a certain way, from the phallic attribution and this "step to be taken" in which the father must offer proof of it, several scenarios reveal an increasing ambiguity where this identity is concerned. It is useful to trace the development of this ambiguity, however concisely, if we want to understand how the transsexual's sexual identity is definitively sustained by a fantasy in which this ambiguity reaches its highest point with regard to the phallic attribution. Let us briefly look at the scenarios of hysteria, homosexuality, fetishism, and transvestism, which seem to form an increasing progression of a considerable ambiguity with regard to challenging the father's phallic attribution.

To begin with the most ordinary aspect of female hysteria, experience shows over and over again that the hysteric willingly enters the phallic dispute and does so in the mode of defiance, especially as a challenge hurled at a man to prove that he really is a man. This can be understood only as a metonymic resurgence of the challenge hurled at the father to prove his virility. As Lucien Israël (1976) puts it, "The paternal lacks that the hysteric seeks to make up for in her choice of partner are imaginary lacks. But they nonetheless designate this partner's role: he is the one who is credited with what the father lacked" (pp. 82–83).

In her phallic demand, the hysteric is often trying to show the father, and men in general, what a "real" man should be like: "Given the nature of her phallic position, she refers to an ideal of the masculine ego only in order to ascertain its lack in her father" (Perrier 1978, p. 66). But in any case, as Lacan astutely observes, "It is only of a woman, after all, that we say that she is manly. . . . Manliness is a woman's matter; she is the only one to believe in it" (1971–1972a, seminar of June 1, 1972).

Most of the time the hysteric's demonstration proceeds in the same way. She has to show a man that it is not enough to have the organ, that is, the penis, in order to be a real man, to be manly. What she does is show the difference between the penis and the phallus, to the point of setting them against one another. Quite commonly such a hysteric reproaches her male partner with not being an adequate man, not because he does not give her pleasure with his penis, but because he might, for example, be unable to protect her in case of danger: although he has the penis, he does not have the phallus. Men are often ready to undertake this demonstration, because they believe themselves to be inadequate. They "actively collaborate in their own condemnation," as Perrier puts it (1978, p. 64). Whatever the result of this testing on the part of the hysteric, and no matter how she exhausts her partner in the phallic competition, it remains the case that the phallus and the organ are always different things. And it is in this way that the respective feminine and masculine identity of the protagonists always remains inscribed in terms of the phallic gift. If we now leave the realm of the neuroses, we shall immediately see how the homosexual woman goes a little further in this same challenge to the phallic attribution. I am following the broad outline of the argument developed by Perrier and Granoff (1979, pp. 175–187).

The homosexual woman cannot renounce "having" the phallus that she "does not have." To be sure, this is also true of the hysteric, but there is a difference revealed by another profile of sexual identity. In contrast to the hysteric, the homosexual woman withdraws from the dialectics of the phallic gift right from the outset. She cannot hope to receive the "gift" of the phallus, since she does not participate in the exchange that becomes established in the heterosexual sphere. But just like the hysteric, in a certain way, she knows where to find the phallus that she does not have: in the one who is not without having it, namely the father.

But although she knows this, she also knows that she is dealing with a father who was never really able to prove that he had it. Here we find the deficit expressed in one of the lesbian's favorite fantasies, in which the father is a man who could never love the mother as he should have done. In her own way, the lesbian also hurls a challenge at the father—and men—regarding the phallic attribution. By way of her sexual identity she is in the best position to sustain this defiance, since, never having had the phallus, she is all the better able to give it. If what is most important is to be able to give the phallus to a woman, the lesbian tries to show a man that she is able to accomplish what none of them can do; since every man is castrated, he can offer a woman only what he does not have.

In order to bring off this demonstration, the homosexual woman "identifies with the insignia of the other" (Perrier and Granoff 1979, p. 84), that is, with the marks of the phallic attribution she was still able to discern in the father. In this way, like a man—if not better than a man, since she does not need a penis—she will bring *jouissance* to a woman and experience *jouissance* through her. The lesbian in a way presents herself as the one who can fill the lack of another woman, and this is the cause of the romantic superiority that she asserts with regard to men, since she herself does not have what is presumed to be the object that fills this lack.

This clearly implies that the lesbian has remained a bit more on this side of castration than the hysteric. Since she does not have it, if she nonetheless tries to demonstrate to men her superiority vis-à-vis women, this is because she remains trapped in the position in which she herself represents the phallus for a woman.

It is still the case, however, that this sexual identity can be sustained only with reference to a male third party. The lesbian invariably has some sort of knowledge about what specifies him as a male, namely the phallus:

> The presence of the masculine third party is apparent not only in the care that this woman will bring to the *jouissance* of her partner—which is a source of pride and glory to her, though in some cases she may systematically neglect the pursuit of her pleasure as agent of the sexual relation—but also in the most trivial association or in dreams, where the male third party, or some object signifying him, seldom fails to appear. [Perrier and Granoff 1979, p. 84]

We have to agree that in homosexuality the distinction between phallus and organ is already a little more unclear than in hysteria.

Let us now take a further step in the disavowal of castration and the challenge to the phallic attribution. This is the step that separates fetishism and transvestism from homosexuality.

If the fetishist, as we have seen, denies the father's phallic attribution to the point of assigning the phallus to the mother, and to all women, via the fetish object, the transvestite goes still further in challenging this attribution. He sets himself up as a fantasmatic representation of what the mother, and the woman, should have. As Perrier and Granoff observe, the transvestite is not, strictly speaking, identified with the mother or the woman, contrary to what some people automatically assume. He places onstage the veil behind which he tends to designate himself, not as a woman, but as the phallus she ought to have. And it is around the problematics of this unveiling that the question of *jouissance* revolves for him, since it is the basis of the sexual excitement he experiences with the anatomical organ that belongs to him. In no case will he do without the presence of this organ, whose unveiling assures his entire *jouissance*.

Here, too, the sexual identity of the transvestite is sustained only by the gaze of the other, summoned as the third party guaranteeing the phallic attribution. And this attribution, even if challenged to its utmost limit through masquerade and deception, is still necessary as the substrate of the sexual identity that the transvestite is trying to sustain.

Whether we are dealing with the hysteric, the lesbian, the fetishist, or the transvestite, each subject's sexual identity is anchored with regard to the phallic attribution. All these scenarios are more or less positioned with regard to castration and hence with regard to the problematics of having. However indirect the routes they take, these subjects achieve the dialectic of the phallic gift. Thus, for example, even if she initially withdraws from it, the homosexual woman at least attempts to give the phallus to another woman, convinced as she is that she will never receive it from a man. The phallic attribution and the circulation of the phallus remain inscribed on the horizon of sexual identity, and this includes the limit case of disavowal in the perversions. This can be so only because of the ongoing distinction, however confused, between the organ and the phallus. On the other hand, as soon as this distinction disappears, the subject is confronted with a sexual identity that is aberrant because it is actually impossible. It is in this impossibility that the transsexual imprisons himself.

17

Transsexualism and the Sex of Angels[1]

The phallic attribution has a direct and decisive effect in the advent of the subject's sexual identity because of the fantasmatic confusion it promotes between the organ and the phallus. This ambiguity reaches its highest point in transsexualism,[2] where it gives rise to a wholly fanciful sexual identity.

From the point of view of the phallic attribution in sexual identity, we are inclined to situate the problematics of the transsexual in the middle ground between the perversions and the psy-

---

1. Many of the main points in this chapter appeared in a condensed form in Dor 1986.

2. I shall not be discussing the medico-legal or juridical aspects of transsexualism, aspects that are properly semiological, or certain etiological and therapeutic considerations. A very systematic report on these different issues is to be found in the report on forensic medicine by Breton and colleagues (1985), which includes a complete bibliography on transsexualism.

choses. Although this is a reasonable hypothesis in view of the phallic logic of psychotics and perverts respectively, it presents certain difficulties depending on whether we are dealing with male or female transsexualism. When it comes to finding reference points, clinical observation suggests a rough estimate that places the male-to-female transsexual on the side of psychotic processes, while the female-to-male is closer to certain perverse processes. Obviously, this is not a nosographic distinction, let alone a structural one. At most it is a supposition that finds some support in what we know about the phallic stakes in the psychoses and the perversions.

MALE TRANSSEXUALISM

While this hypothesis can verify some theoretical and clinical arguments, we first have to take a preliminary look at some orthodox accounts of transsexual psychopathology. By far the most extensive treatment is that of Robert J. Stoller (1975), who devotes a major part of his study *Sex and Gender* to transsexualism. Without going into Stoller's detailed theory of the relationship between sexual identity and transsexualism, we can trace the broad outlines of this impressive clinical account. (Here I am following the brilliant studies by Kress-Rosen 1982, pp. 13–17, and, in a more concise version, Millot 1983, Ch. 4.)

Stoller's initial concern seems to be to define the structural landmarks of transsexualism with reference to the sexual identities that are close to it: homosexuality and transvestism. One distinction between transsexuals and homosexuals (transvestites or not) seems to be based on the criterion of one's sense of identity. Homosexuals and transvestites make believe they are women while continuing to feel that they are men, but this is not the case with transsexuals.

A second distinction seems to be the different relation to the penis. Homosexuals and transvestites clearly derive sexual pleasure from their organ, whereas transsexuals experience the presence of their penis with the greatest horror. In fact, the transsexual feels that he is a woman, and he lives as a woman. This explains why he never feels that he is in a homosexual position when in a relationship with men. He likes men because he considers himself a female partner. Nor does he consider himself to be a transvestite when he is dressed as a woman.

Beyond this sense of feminine identity there is another characteristic feature, namely the very specific connection transsexuals had with their mothers in childhood. Although they are "children whose unambiguous assignment to the male sex was made at birth and never questioned" (Kress-Rosen, p. 13), they exhibit feminine behaviors from very early on. It is truly as though "the essence of the transsexual is his mother" (Millot, p. 48).

One of the typical features of the mother–child relation in these cases is the close connection on the bodily level, a connection that soon becomes an ongoing "body-to-body" contact. Mother and child are never apart, even to sleep. The child, always close to the mother's body, constantly needs to return to it in order to be touched. Any physical separation is all but impossible. This closeness is by and large promoted by the irrelevance of the father, who barely exists for both of them and remains radically external to the mother–child symbiosis. Thus mother and child share a mutual love that nothing will threaten: he is everything for her, and she is everything for him.

It is interesting to compare this type of mother–child relation to other, apparently similar, ones and especially to recall the contrast Stoller emphasizes with the relation of future homosexuals with their mothers. Though the mother of the homosexual also has a close relation with her child, in the case of this and other perversions she always traps the child in a fundamental ambiguity. This consists in keeping the child dependent on an erotic seduction while making quite sure he is aware of the threat of castration from a symbolic position that she herself has usurped.

The mother of the transsexual, on the other hand, loves her child beyond any seduction and ambivalence. Since the father's influence is entirely nonexistent, nothing is ever played out in the register of having. The mother does not present herself as lacking the phallic attribute: the child simply *is* her phallus. This being the case, we might be inclined to think of the kind of mother–child relation that leads to psychosis. But Stoller denies that this could be the outcome. As Kress-Rosen puts it, "Stoller refers to this relation as symbiotic, and yet he claims that it is unlike the relation that unites the schizophrenic's mother with her child, since there is no source of suffering here, no double bind" (p. 13). Moreover, "Stoller sets aside psychosis from the outset, on the grounds that the subject's social skills remain intact" (p. 14).

In addition to the fact that these few clinical arguments advanced by Stoller with regard to psychosis are rather tenuous, his theory of the development of sexual identity only increases the difficulty. Stoller is of the opinion that the sole authentic transsexualism is the male kind. This is actually the major point in his theorization, which, based on some data from contemporary biology, posits a primary femininity that underlies all identities. From this perspective, masculine identity results from a subsequent process of psychic masculinization. The question, then, is this: How can one become a man following the symbiotic state in which the child is inscribed in a feminine identification? The transsexual, in this view, is someone who does not manage to overcome primary femininity.

Sexual identity is said to be constituted in several stages. The first is that of primary femininity regardless of the child's sex, and this is sustained and maintained by the necessarily symbiotic relation between mother and child in the first months of life. The child cannot help identifying with the mother who is taking care of him and making sure that his needs are met. The second stage, according to Stoller, ends in core gender identity. It is constituted by environmental influences that designate the child as a boy or a girl. This stage may mark the beginning of the child's psychic masculinization by gradually undoing his fusional relation with his mother. This core gender identity is "an inalienable foundation that will persist during all later vicissitudes of identification (Millot, p. 53), inevitably positioning the child as a man or a woman. Stoller's third stage is that of the Oedipus, radically distinguished from the preceding stages by the intrusion of the conflict the child comes to experience with his mother and his father. Nevertheless it confirms, even as it exploits, the gender identity acquired earlier.

All this clearly implies that only the second stage represents a crucial moment in the development of sexual identity. The transsexual process is thus the result of a symbiotic relation between mother and child that continues in spite of everything, with no challenge to this primal identification in later stages. In other words, nothing intervenes in a decisive manner to signify and produce a masculine core gender identity.

This theory of sexual identity is open to a number of substantial criticisms supported by clinical observation. One line of critique is proposed by Nicolle Kress-Rosen (1982) in connection with the distinction masculinity / femininity. According to Kress-Rosen, Stoller is trapped in phenomenological clichés and ideological behaviors. For him, she states, "a woman is a subject who behaves in a feminine way, who likes to get dressed up, attend to her home, and raise children, and, in contrast, a male is any subject who is interested in a career, likes fixing things, and engages in violent sports" (p. 14). These cultural reference points confirm Stoller's victimization by the ideological masquerade and the make-believe that underlie his concepts of masculinity and femininity.

Kress-Rosen makes an additional point that seems to contradict some of Stoller's observations. If we agree that future transsexuals fiercely identify with their mothers' femininity, we can understand why these children soon begin to exhibit typically feminine behaviors and appearances. But how are we to understand this early imitation given the fact that most of these mothers are usually quite restrained from this point of view? It is hard to explain how little boys come to behave like little girls while their mothers are conspicuous for the opposite attitude.

A second and more fundamental line of argument concerns the issue of the phallus and castration in Stoller's etiological approach to transsexualism (cf. Kress-Rosen, pp. 14–15). Although Stoller isolates this structure from psychotic structures and makes distinctions between them, he does not take into account the problematics of the phallic attribution and castration. If, as he notes, the child is treated by the mother as an extension of her own body, he is therefore unquestionably her phallus. But though he conceptualizes and formulates matters in this way, and includes the phallic problematics in the genesis of transsexualism, he does not draw the essential conclusion, namely the fact that the child will necessarily have to locate himself in the field of maternal desire with regard to this third term that is the phallic object.

Catherine Millot (1983, pp. 54–56) offers a complementary line of argument. Stoller's notion of symbiosis is that of the biologist. But Millot aptly remarks that the mother–infant relation is of another order: "Oneness with the mother is a fantasy that is constructed retroactively, on the basis of a loss, a separation that has always already taken place" (p. 54). We have to presuppose lack and castration with regard to the mother's desire before the child is invested as her phallus and maintained as such. The very nature of these problematics challenges the idea of a symbiosis.

Moreover, any identification with the phallus presupposes the Other to whom the child addresses his demands. In making demands, he inevitably encounters the dimension of lack. The mother cannot fail to appear as this Other from the beginning, introducing the child to the alterity that he will constantly refuse to accept by elaborating the fantasy of maternal omnipotence. The child's primary identification as phallic is always an identification with this omnipotence.

In any case, Stoller's use of the concept of the phallus calls for a much more rigorous examination of this phallic logic in transsexual dynamics.

A further clinical remark is in order concerning Stoller's notion of a sense of identity. Contrary to what Stoller claims, transsexuals are in no way convinced that they feel like women in men's bodies. As early as his first studies, recorded in his 1956 thesis in medicine, J.-M. Alby determined that transsexuals incontestably feel themselves to be men because they have a penis. As Marcel Czermak (1982) correctly reminds us, "It is in the face of the failure, the inadequacy, of an imaginary identification that they ask for a real sanction as soon as they are approached as men" (p. 19). Insofar as the transsexual hopes to look like a woman, we are always dealing with something on the order of appearance and masquerade. As Czermak notes, the transsexual "tends to reduce himself to this masquerade. He is the masquerade, the envelope and claim for bodily transformation" (p. 14). In other words, the transsexual is concerned less with being *a* woman than with being Woman as such. This is what Kress-Rosen means when she speaks of "the frantic idealization of femininity" (p. 15).

This idealization knows no limit, since it must be inscribed on the body with the extreme care for perfection needed to sustain an appearance that is always subordinated to norms of moral purity. And it is an established fact that a good number of transsexuals refuse any sexual intercourse until they have been transformed into women; they have no further relations with women if they are married and no homosexual relations with men.

Czermak's clinical observations bear out this concern for moral purity linked to the ideal of femininity. He reports the case of a transsexual who asked him for a certificate of anal virginity. Another highly significant clinical observation of this idealized femininity purged of all moral taint is that many postoperative transsexuals refuse vaginal construction so as never to be compromised by the intolerable and degrading nature of sexual life (cf. Czermak, p. 19). The only thing that seems to matter is the appearance of being a woman, the ideal woman of their dreams, with the necessary corollary of being without a sex. There is no more consummate fantasy than seeking to embody the angelic position, that is, the position of Woman who resembles a Name-of-the-Father, as we have seen (Chapter 16).

Contrary to Stoller's thesis, it seems clear that the transsexual is in no way exempt from the imperatives of castration and phallic problematics. He is nonetheless closer to the psychotic mode than to that of neurosis. For example, while the hysteric is worn out by the unconscious question, "Am I a man? / Am I a woman?" in the name of his or her phallic claim, the transsexual never reaches the point of asking a question like, "What is a woman?" He has no uncertainty on this matter and knows the answer in advance: a woman is what he wants to be!

Although neurotics and perverts are absorbed in conjectures as imaginary as they are symptomatic on the question of their sexual identity, we know that only symbolic castration can bring some surcease to this fantasmatic torment. The transsexual withdraws right away from this imaginary back-and-forth, trapped as he is by the real of his sexual anatomy. Thus the only castration to which he seems to have access is the surgical castration that involves the suppression of the organ.

This being the case, how are we to understand his relation to the phallic signifier? For him, phallic problematics do not come into play so as to govern his relation to sex and sexual identity, and this is so because, since the transsexual has no access to the phallic signifier, the question of his sexual identity remains firmly limited to the anatomical level. He is thus trapped in the dimension of being, and hence we find the closeness to psychotic processes.

This proximity of male transsexuals to the psychoses is reminiscent of what Lacan liked to call "the push to the woman" in psychosis. Clinical observation bears out the idea that feminization can be identified in several psychotic symptom pictures, and the position of the male transsexual may well find some solid confirmation in this regard. In this context, we are bound to recall one of President Schreber's favorite fantasies: "If it is such a uniquely beautiful thing for him to be a woman, this is because what he wants to be is the wife of God" (Kress-Rosen, p. 15).

Lacanian theory may be able to shed further light on this kinship between male transsexualism and the psychoses. Here a hypothesis proposed by Catherine Millot (1983, Ch. 3) is worth mentioning, however briefly. According to Millot, if we consider the Other as not castrated (the at-least-one who had all the women), he can be identified with the father of the primal horde and hence with the symbolic father. If Woman can be said to exist, she functions as this Name-of-the-Father, the referent of a *jouissance* as absolute as it is forbidden, and it could be said of her: $\exists x \, \overline{\Phi x}$.

Moreover, we know that the identification with such an allpowerful Other is the child's archaic phallic identification. If nothing mediates it, it remains captive, prey to the mechanism that leads to psychotic processes. How can the entrapment in phallic identification make a subject want to become a woman, as the transsexual tries to do, and not lead to psychosis? Certain theses of Lacan's enable us to explore this issue, if only by suggesting an explanatory hypothesis about male transsexualism. Millot argues that, in transsexualism, something does indeed intervene to set a limit to the *jouissance* of the Other, in the sense that the signifier Woman can function as the signifier Name-of-the-Father. In support of this hypothesis, she refers to Lacan's metaphoric algorithm of the Borromean knot.

The Borromean knot is a figure composed of three interlocking rings such that, if one is broken, the two others are unlinked. Lacan used it as a metaphor for the way in which, in the unconscious, the Symbolic, the Imaginary, and the Real are connected for the subject. The distinctive property of the Borromean knot can be extended to an infinite number of other rings without losing its fundamental nature: the breaking of one ring frees all the others. Lacan also uses a four-ring knot to show how, in the Oedipus, the ring Name-of-the-Father binds the three registers of the Symbolic, the Imaginary, and the Real. If the ring Name-of-the-Father is missing, the knotting of Symbolic, Imaginary, and Real cannot hold firm.

Millot offers an analogous explanation for the transsexual position. The absence of the Name-of-the-Father is compensated for by the signifier of the impossible Woman, which maintains structure by introducing a limit. Yet this fourth element, Woman, will never manage more than to hold together the Imaginary and the Symbolic: the Real will remain free. This is why the transsexual man's demand for surgical correction appears as a way to adjust the Real of the genital to the Imaginary and the Symbolic. It is through this correction and this replacement that psychosis is avoided.

On this last point—the avoidance of psychosis—Czermak (1982) takes a clinical position more detailed than Millot's: "This woman the transsexual wants to become, this term "woman" that he attributes to whatever is endowed with beauty, unity, completeness, the universal mother all in one, this woman appears as Woman, one of the Names-of-the-Father, which finally convinced me of the psychotic nature of what we are dealing with" (p. 22). According to Czermak, in paranoid psychosis there is a feminizing aspect. In his view, a transsexual potential exists in all psychosis in the form of what we are accustomed to call psychotic homosexuality. Transsexualism is thus one of the forms in which psychosis crystallizes.

Though of course the question remains open, this hypothesis sheds light on the ethics of corrective intervention. Such intervention is, in some way, just the realization of a delusional idea, as Alby (1956) notes. The problem is to know whether this surgical correction does or does not have a calming therapeutic effect. Though some postoperative transsexuals claim to feel better, clinical observation tends to show the contrary. Most of them admit that they live a hellish existence marked by a dissatisfaction that often leads to substance abuse and suicide. Surgical correction tends to be beneficial for transsexuals only to the extent that it removes the fear of being unmasked as women; it does not settle the question of the deadly *jouissance* that continues to torment them. Most often it is even a catalyst for the decompensation of these subjects. It is, in fact, an intervention whose therapeutic effect is limited to satisfying the delusional demand of a subject. Ethically, the problem increases with the whole issue of the legal change of identity.

The least we can say is that the juridical situation of transsexuals is completely ambiguous. A substantial juridical measure is surely desirable to counteract the uncontrolled activity of surgeons. The question is what these measures should be: to suppress the intervention and legally forbid the changing of sex, or to authorize it? The current tendency favors the second solution on the grounds of the supposedly therapeutic nature of corrective surgery, and juridical opinion remains dependent, to some extent, on this weighty therapeutic supposition. It is all the weightier because, in the long term, there would appear to be no difference between postoperative transsexuals and the others. In other words, surgery seems to be at most a palliative measure, but one that does not cure a disturbance that is essentially psychopathological.

FEMALE TRANSSEXUALISM

From Stoller's point of view, the etiology of female transsexualism is as problematical as in the case of the male. It is likewise based on the theory of a primal femininity resulting from the symbiosis of the child and her mother, except that, in the present case, we must account for the origin of masculine identification. This presupposes—still in the context of Stoller's logic—that an early and overriding paternal influence must counteract primal femininity.

Stoller's idea is that female transsexuals did not have a satisfactory symbiotic experience because it was counteracted too soon. He cites as evidence depressed and ill mothers who were unable to take care of their young child. Their unavailability is said to have favored a highly charged paternal presence that led to an early masculine identification substituting for the experience of primary femininity and the identification with the mother that underlies it. In this view the little girl, identified with a male model, feels her first sexual stirrings as a function of this identity, experiencing herself as a boy with other girls. As a result, we find the same disposition with regard to homosexuality: identified with a male, the future female transsexual in no way considers herself a lesbian.

Typical corrections of a morphological, surgical, and endocrine nature are sought with the onset of the puberty that the transsexual experiences so tragically:

> Puberty and menarche are dramatically resented. She binds her chest, both to prevent her breasts from growing and to conceal their outline under her shirt. As often as possible they dress as what they feel like—a man—and pass as such with girls they hope to win. On a regular basis they construct an artificial penis out of cloth or rubber that makes an appropriate bulge in their pants and is sometimes sturdy enough to function. [Millot 1983, p. 102]

These alterations allow them to function socially as men (with much more ease, incidentally, than their male counterparts). Some of them obtain a change of civil status and marry women with whom they have children by artificial insemination.

Stoller's hypothesis about female transsexualism, then, is essentially based on the idea of the predominance of symbiosis with the father and on the importance of early conditioning that encourages the child in the direction of masculinity. His argument here suffers from the same weaknesses as the argument regarding male transsexualism and is open to same kinds of criticism. On the other hand, the specificity of the feminine transsexual position calls for clarification of the similarity and the difference between it and the two perverse scenarios of the transvestite and the lesbian.

As Millot aptly notes, there is a feature of transvestism that precisely defines one of the components of the *jouissance* proper to this perversion. This is the sexual arousal produced by wearing the clothing of the opposite sex. Here we obviously have a crucial element of the perverse process: *jouissance* associated with the gaze of the Other when presented with the revelation of the hoax. From this point of view, transvestism is an authentic and exclusively male perversion.

Clearly, this *jouissance* of transvestites dressed as women is not found in women dressed as men. As well as posing a very serious question about the existence of a perverse structure in women, does this mean, as in Stoller's hasty conclusion, that every woman who permanently dresses as a man is a transsexual? It is one thing to take note of the fact that female transsexualism probably does not occur as a perversion, another to decide that, in the absence of the element of sexual arousal, every woman who regularly dresses as a man is a transsexual.

It is true that the absence of sexual arousal is common in these women. This raises the whole issue of the distinction to be made between female transsexualism and female homosexuality. The homosexual woman dressed as a man clearly feels no particular *jouissance* in her choice of clothing. But this does not make her a transsexual. To get a better understanding of this difference, let us note a striking distinction between male and female transsexuals. The male transsexual puts in the foreground of what Alby calls his delusional conviction the fact of appearing to be a woman, to be Woman, but in no way to desire as a woman. Moreover, we have seen that this desiring dimension is often absent in male transsexuals, who are usually horrified at the thought of sexual intercourse. In contrast, with female transsexuals the female sexual object is often the occasion for a constant and early libidinal investment. Thus there is a feature of identity that places female transsexualism somewhat near female homosexuality. Some clinicians have even referred to this identity in arguing for female transsexualism as a disavowal of homosexuality, that is, as a defense.

But this view is very hard to accept. Though it is true that there is a gap between male and female transsexualism, the two share at least the identification with the phallus. In both cases this phallic identification is designed to neutralize the signifier of sexual difference. Thus male and female transsexuals have in common their eagerness to efface the marks of that difference on their own bodies. The man has himself emasculated and the woman proposes to have her breasts, ovaries, and uterus removed: each tries to suppress the concrete signs of the sexual difference that reminds them of their incompleteness by hindering their phallic identification.

But we still have to understand why the identification with the phallus does not always lead to transsexualism. For example, let us juxtapose female transsexualism and female homosexuality. In certain respects, the problematics of female transsexualism involve the same stakes that we find in the hysteric and the lesbian: the undermining of the father's phallic attribution through the challenge to his virility. Like the lesbian and the hysteric, the female transsexual tries to show the father what a real man is. Yet this demonstration is different in each case.

As we have seen, the hysteric, who is perfectly able to distinguish the phallus from the organ, most often tries to set them against one another in order to show that virility can indeed do without the organ. For her part, the lesbian tries to show a man how a woman should be loved by giving what one does not have to a partner who does not have it either. Thus it is not enough to give what one has (the penis). The lesbian proves that a man is unable to give a woman what he does not have. In both cases, we determined that these fantasmatic strategies are sustained only to the extent that the phallus and the organ are always fundamentally distinct, which leaves a path open to the dialectic of the phallic gift.

In contrast, it is as though the female transsexual cannot gain access to this dialectic because she confuses the organ with the phallus as the signifier of sexual difference. In this sense, the transsexual woman seems to succumb to the same deception as her male counterpart, namely reducing the phallic signifier to the organ it-self. Moreover, just as the male transsexual tries to be identified with Woman, the female tries to identify with *a* man. Both cases involve taking up the challenge of an impossible identification. And it is precisely this impossibility that they try to counteract by a sex change in reality. But despite this intervention in the anatomical real of the sexes, such subjects are still assigned to a position "out-side of sex," as Lacan put it.

For in fact, the phallus is the signifier of sexual difference. Try-ing to identify with the phallic signifier, therefore, amounts to try-ing to embody the middle ground that is difference itself. Now, it is just this middle ground of difference that, on both sides of the phal-lic signifier, determines two sexuations. Because it is necessarily "outside of sex," the incarnation of the phallus as support for a pos-sible sexual identity thus involves trying to incarnate the fantasy of the sex of angels. As Lacan observes, transsexuals are the victims of a mistake that involves confusing the organ and the signifier, a quasi-delusional error that leads them to harbor the conviction that in getting rid of the organ they will reject the signifier.

Nevertheless, in spite of the common adherence to this delu-sional conviction, there is a radical asymmetry between male and female transsexuals. This asymmetry is, if not obscure, at least subtle on account of the obsessive tendency that transsexuals of both sexes share with the same eagerness: no matter what, it is essential *to ap-pear like* the sex one has chosen as the norm of one's sexual identity. The mirage they constantly maintain in order to heighten this ap-pearance is obviously dependent on a lack of symbolic support, which, as Millot (1983) observes, "leads to falling back on the imagi-nary and a corresponding inflation of ideals" (p. 114). In order to sculpt the image of their bodily ideal through whatever surgical modifications they choose, these pariahs of appearance exhaust them-selves trying to perfect their imaginary membership in an impossible sexual identity. This just shows the infinite extent of the tribute they have to pay to the phallic signifier.

It is with regard to this debt that male and female transsexuals seem to differ. Trapped in their archaic phallic identification, male transsexuals become enclosed in the domain of being the phallus at the price of the real emasculation they prescribe for themselves, the irreversible scars of which represent their point of no return with regard to symbolic castration and the assumption of sexual difference that governs it. This irreversible assignation more or less condemns them to an almost inevitable immigration into the ghetto of the psychoses.

The ambivalence of the hysterical woman concerning her own sexual identity is most often expressed in her ceaseless interrogation of femininity. This insistent questioning can, via displacement, find temporary relief in the fantasy of the bodily modification that "would adjust their image to their ideal" (Millot, p. 114). This is the ordinary fate of starlets who submit to the often disastrous results of plastic surgery. A similar influence of the imaginary is found in the dynamic of the unconscious identification with the man that is revealed in the phallic claim, or what Adler called the masculine protest, of hysterics.

The passage to female homosexuality gives this masculine demand a more querulous tone, insofar as homosexuality is based on defiance and on the substrate of the disavowal of castration that is proper to perversion.

Female transsexuals, too, have to inscribe themselves in the list of these different scenarios, scenarios in which the phallic claim finds its logical progression in an imaginary quest that gets more and more embroiled in the register of having. Seeking to conform as best she can to the image of the man that haunts her, all the transsexual can ever do is embody this masculine claim to the most extreme point, incarnating it on and in the real of her body. Kress-

Rosen (1982) rightly emphasizes the tendency of female trans-sexuals to cling to the domain of having:

> When they disguise themselves as men, they want to be rec-ognized as such and pursue the masquerade to the point of getting a transplant in a series of painful interventions, though it always remains a prosthesis. They remain in the domain of having, losing precisely what made them phallic. Thus they always move in the register of penis envy, but with the dis-turbing intrusion of the real in their demand, which never-theless suggests that the passage to transsexualism from the positions of masculine claim, even of active homosexuality, a passage that would seem to occur in a straight line, never occurs except in very serious cases. [p. 16]

It is as though, in contrast to male transsexuals alienated in an almost psychotic demand for being the phallus, female trans-sexuals are located on the side of the need to have it that is also at work in the perversions. At this point, we still have to explain the ambiguity raised by the problem of female perversion itself.

Conclusion:
Perversion and Perverse Women

Outside of the homosexuality in which they can become involved, it seems risky, not to mention irresponsible, to speak of sexual perversions in women. This does not mean that women cannot have a certain relation to perversion. But beside these affinities, can we demonstrate a dynamic of desire in women that meets the structural criteria defining perversion in men?

Let us begin with the exemplary case of female homosexuality. In addition to the phallic dynamic that is actualized in the manner we have discussed (cf. Chapter 16), let us consider the reference to the masculine third party in the homosexual relation. This reference, implicit or explicit, is constantly evoked for the sole reason that the masculine third party is always presumed to be invested with phallic emblems. Moreover, Perrier and Granoff (1979, p. 84) point out the concern with this phallic attribution in the romantic relation of the lesbian and her partner, namely in the care she takes to assure the partner's *jouissance* as she imagines a man can do with a woman because of his phallic attributes.

And this reference to a masculine third party, an inevitable sign of the challenge that the lesbian hurls at every man insofar as he is castrated, has an additional interest. For the mediation of this third party indirectly raises the question of the very essence of femininity underlying the whole enigmatic issue of female perversion.

In a remarkable study, Piera Aulagnier (1967a) examines the question of femininity at the very point where the pervert's tragic interrogation is constituted in the face of the discovery of the absence of the mother's penis. Defining castration as the lack that makes the object of desire emerge into the foreground, Aulagnier finds in this missing object the point at which femininity arises, femininity being "the name given by the subject of desire to the object in the place where it cannot be named because it is missing" (p. 69).

The establishment of this reference point, entirely based on the fertile moment that Freud mentions in his paper on femininity (1932), has the immediate result of subordinating the field of femininity to the recognition of the other. Thus only the other can bring a woman some assurance on the question of her femininity. In other words, a woman never receives the investiture of her femininity except by the consent of a man, whose desire alone signifies whether or not she possesses it. And Aulagnier confirms this argument *a contrario*, recalling the extreme vigilance with which every woman examines her body for the least sign of virility.

On the other hand, the assumption of this femininity invariably leads to a rivalry of every woman with every other, thereby validating the term *envy* that Freud specifies as a constant in feminine structure. As Aulagnier very aptly puts it, "femininity, from the moment it arises, shares with the penis the privilege of being *par excellence* the object of envy" (p. 70). With the register of envy we return, via femininity, to the problematics of female homosexuality and perversion. Penis envy, in its metonymic form of phallic demand, is the lesbian's paradoxical expression of the envy of the femininity that she venerates in her partner. The partner is all the more the object of this homosexual coveting if she presents herself as a potential object of attraction to a man.

This is indirect confirmation of the idea that an ambiguous dialectic of desire underlies the perverse processes. Hence the paradox noted by Perrier and Granoff (1979, pp. 85–86) in connection with the lesbian's archaic libidinal investment. At first glance, the lesbian seems to have loved her father too much. But, before this, she had loved her mother too much and could not endure the frustration of this love. On the occasion of the pre-oedipal change of object, the father inherits the transferred love and becomes the support of a possible masculine identification. The paternal love object disappears as such only because the child introjects him and thereby appropriates his phallic insignia. And it happens that the mother's discourse constantly reveals that the father has never been able to make use of these phallic emblems as far as she is concerned. In thus signifying herself to her daughter as lacking, the mother is also disclosing the imposture of the father, who supposedly had the phallus but was unable to "lay down the law." The ambiguity is often enough to lead the girl to identify with the object of this lack. Thus Perrier and Granoff observe that "when a subject takes on the insignia of what he is identified with, he is transformed and becomes the signifier of these insignia" (p. 85).

This is true of the homosexual woman. In offering herself as an object that can fill the lack in the other, she renews her first love in a certain way, unconsciously finding in the other the mother who lacks. She can do this all the better since she herself represents the object of this lack that she does not have, but that she can nevertheless give to the female other. This is the feat that the lesbian sets out to accomplish with regard to what no man (no father) could do.

Although homosexuality is a possible sexual pathway for women, can we still speak of perversion? The case is rather that the woman actualizes her libidinal investment in a perverse mode without ever having anything to pervert.

If, in terms of the specification of a structure, the problem of perversion makes sense only with regard to sexual perversions, we can at most conclude that some women actualize individual, favorably orchestrated, elements of male perversions. To mention only the disavowal of castration as the most fundamental feature underlying the perverse structure, we must admit that this specific trait is completely recessive in the woman's economy of desire. Although castration concerns the woman as much as it does the man, she does not question it except insofar as it threatens and marks the other whom she desires. This, as Perrier and Granoff observe, is one of the "privileges of the girl with respect to the law" (p. 92). When it comes to the other privileges, the woman reveals an aptitude not for becoming perverted herself but for "perverting her libido" (p. 90), either through narcissism or through excessive mothering.

Thus, without being a fetishist, the woman can always become fetishized. This is one of the most exemplary scenarios in the perversion of narcissism. The woman becomes her own fetish by offering her body for the sexual *jouissance* of a man. But the erotization of the body-fetish is satisfactory only on condition that this body is yielded to a man, deprived of its phallic attribution and the reference to the law that it presupposes—that is to say, if the body is reduced to an instrumental function pure and simple. This explains why certain women tend to have ill-considered sexual relations not only with numerous men but men who are totally unlike them. The random nature of these experiences, constantly renewed and perceived as nymphomania, usually leaves other women amazed, uneasy, and dumbfounded. This reaction is understandable in view of the fact that the spectacular aspect of the fetishization of the body offered to all comers is mostly a solid defense against homosexuality.

As for excessive mothering, Perrier and Granoff emphasize the perverse nature of the relation that a mother can establish with her child if sublimation does not take place. In particular, there can be a veritable erotomania expressed through the access to the child's body that inevitably accompanies the satisfaction of his needs. In this perverse maternal disposition, the child inevitably encounters an echo to the dynamics of his desire, and this leads him to constitute himself as the object that fills the lack in the Other. If the father's mediation is inadequate, taking the form of a silent collusion, the mother entraps the child in the kind of seduction we have discussed.

In her study of femininity, Aulagnier (1967a) presents another scenario that must be viewed as a perversion of the libido. Starting from the fact that a woman often harbors the fantasy of being the object of passion of the other whom she loves, Aulagnier writes that "women's special attraction to passion can serve as a port of entry to the register of the perversions" (p. 62). In the name of this ideal goal of being the sole desire, the only one to be a vital need for the other, the female dynamic of desire may become perverted. This potential disposition is illustrated by a canonical example of female masochism, the prostitution fantasy.

Aulagnier notes that this fantasy primarily stems from the mutual interaction of transgression and submission. The more the female object is mistreated and rejected, the more she is invested as an object that bestows *jouissance*. Hence the prostitute manages to combine the feminine masochistic position with the paradigmatic object of *jouissance*. She tends to occupy the place of the object of lack that provides *jouissance*, thereby signifying that a woman embodies the very proof of a victory over castration. In her submission to the every need of her partner, she affords him the fantasy that he lacks nothing. She thereby becomes the sole and unique satisfaction of the desire of the other. It is through this masochistic fantasy of prostitution that a woman's desire becomes perverted into passion.

But, whatever the manifestations of perversion in a woman, we are not entitled to speak of perverse processes organized on the level of a structure. At most what we can do is identify in perverse behavior the traces of infantile polymorphous perversion that may allow a woman to offer herself as an instrument in the service of a man's perversion.

In fact, because of the relation that the woman necessarily maintains with the real of phallic absence, her perverse manifestations are difficult to ascribe to sexual perversion in the strict sense, if we give this term the specifically structural connotation that Freud and his followers have defined. From this point of view, it seems that we must accept the consequences entailed by this notion of structure and admit that "outside of homosexuality, the path along which female sexuality can become engaged but not perverted, . . . there are no perversions properly speaking in women" (Perrier and Granoff 1979, p. 89).

References

Alby, J.-M. (1956). *Contribution à l'Etude du Transsexualisme. Thesis in Medicine.* Paris.

Aulagnier, P. (1964). Remarques sur la structure psychotique. *La Psychanalyse* 8. Paris, PUF.

———— (1967a). Remarques sur la féminité et ses avatars. In *Le Désir et la Perversion.* Paris: Seuil.

———— (1967b). La perversion comme structure. *L'Inconscient* 2:11–41. Paris: PUF.

Ball, B. (1888). *La Folie Erotique.* Paris: Baillère.

Bardenat, C. (1975). Articles "Perversité" and "Perversion" in *Manuel Alphabétique de Psychiatrie*, ed. A. Porot. Paris: PUF.

Breton, J., Frowirth, C., and Pottiez, S., eds. (1985). *Le Transsexualisme, Etude Nosographique et Médico-Légale.* Paris: Masson.

Clavreul, J. (1967). Le couple pervers. In *Le Désir et la Perversion.* Paris: Seuil.

———— (1985). Perversions. In *Encyclopaedia Universalis*, vol. 14. Paris.

Czermak, M. (1982). Précisions cliniques sur le transsexualisme. *Le discours Psychanalytique* 3.

Dor, J. (1985). *Introduction to the Reading of Lacan: The Unconscious Structured Like a Language*, ed. J. F. Gurewich and S. Fairfield. New York: Other Press, 2000.

———— (1986). Identité sexuelle et transsexualisme. *Esquisses psychanalytiques* 6:69–79.

Ellis, H. (1905–1942). *Studies in the Psychology of Sex.* New York: Random House.

Ey, H. (1950). *Etudes Psychiatriques* 13:238–246. Paris: Desclée de Brouwer.

Freud, S. (1893–1895). Studies on hysteria. *Standard Edition* 2.

———— (1905a). Jokes and their relation to the unconscious. *Standard Edition* 8.

———— (1905b). Three essays on the theory of sexuality. *Standard Edition* 7:123–243.

———— (1908a). On the sexual theories of children. *Standard Edition* 9:205–226.

———— (1908b). Character and anal erotism. *Standard Edition* 9:167–175.

———— (1910). "Wild" psycho-analysis. *Standard Edition* 11:219–227.

———— (1912). Recommendations to physicians practicing psycho-analysis. *Standard Edition* 12:109–120.

———— (1912–1913). Totem and taboo. *Standard Edition* 13:1–161.

———— (1913a). On beginning the treatment. *Standard Edition* 12:121–144.

———— (1913b). The disposition to obsessional neurosis. *Standard Edition* 12:311–326.

———— (1915). Instincts and their vicissitudes. *Standard Edition* 14:109–140.

———— (1917). On transformation of instinct as exemplified in anal erotism. *Standard Edition* 17:125–133.

———— (1921). Group psychology and the analysis of the ego. *Standard Edition* 18:65–143.

———— (1923). The infantile genital organization. *Standard Edition* 19:139–145.

———— (1924a). Neurosis and psychosis. *Standard Edition* 19:147–153.

———— (1924b). The loss of reality in neurosis and psychosis. *Standard Edition* 19:81–187.

———— (1925). Some psychical consequences of the anatomical distinction between the sexes. *Standard Edition* 19:241–258.

———— (1927). Fetishism. *Standard Edition* 21:147–157.

———— (1932). Femininity. *Standard Edition* 22:112–135.

———— (1939). An outline of psycho-analysis. *Standard Edition* 23:139–207.

Gessain, R. (1957). *Vagina dentata* dans la clinique et la mythologie. In *La Psychanalyse*, vol. 3, pp. 247–295. Paris: PUF.

Israël, L. (1976). *L'Hystérique, le Sexe et le Médecin*. Paris: Masson.

Jung, K. G. (1911). *Psychology of the Unconscious. A Study of the Transformations and Symbolisms of the Libido*, trans. B. R. Hinkle. Princeton, NJ: Princeton University Press.

Juranville, A. (1984). *Lacan et la Philosophie*. Paris: PUF.

Krafft-Ebing, R. von. (1869). *Psychopathia Sexualis*, trans. F. J. Rebman. London: Rebman.

Kress-Rosen, N. (1982). Introduction à la question du transsexualisme. *Le Discours Psychanalytique* 3.

Lacan, J. (1953). The function and field of speech and language in psychoanalysis. In *Ecrits. A Selection*, trans. A. Sheridan, pp. 30–113. New York: Norton, 1977.

———— (1955–1956). *The Seminar. Book III. The Psychoses*, trans. R. Grigg. New York: Norton, 1992.

———— (1956). Situation de la psychanalyse et formation du psychanalyste en 1956. In *Ecrits*, pp. 459–491. Paris: Seuil.

———— (1957a). The agency of the letter in the unconscious or reason since Freud. In *Ecrits. A Selection*, trans. A. Sheridan, pp. 146–178. New York: Norton, 1977.

———— (1957b). On a question preliminary to any possible treatment of psychosis. In *Ecrits. A Selection*, trans. A. Sheridan, pp. 179–225. New York: Norton, 1977.

———— (1957–1958). *Le séminaire. Livre V. Les formations de l'inconscient.* Unpublished.

———— (1960). Subversion of the subject and the dialectic of desire in the Freudian unconscious. In *Ecrits. A Selection*, trans. A. Sheridan, pp. 292–325. New York: Norton, 1977.

———— (1962). Kant avec Sade, trans. J. B. Swenson. *October* 51:55–75, 1989.

———— (1969–1970). *Le séminaire. Livre XVII. L'envers de la psychanalyse.* Unpublished.

————— (1970–1971). *Le séminaire. Livre XVIII. D'un discours qui ne serait pas du semblant.* Unpublished.

————— (1971–1972a). *Le savoir du psychanalyste.* Unpublished.

————— (1971–1972b). *Le séminaire. Livre XIX. . . . Ou pire.* Unpublished.

————— (1972). L'Etourdit. *Scilicet* 4:5–52, 1973.

————— (1972–1973). *On Feminine Sexuality, The Limits of Love and Knowledge. Encore. The Seminar of Jacques Lacan. Book XX*, ed. J.-A. Miller, trans. B. Fink. New York: Norton, 1998.

Laplanche, J., and Pontalis, J.-B. (1973). *The Language of Psycho-Analysis*, trans. D. Nicholson-Smith. New York: Norton.

Lwoff, A. (1970). *Biological Order.* Cambridge, MA: MIT Press.

Mannoni, M. (1965). *Le Premier Rendez-vous avec le Psychanalyste.* Paris: Denoël.

Mannoni, O. (1969). *Clefs pour l'Imaginaire, ou l'Autre Scène.* Paris: Seuil.

Melman, C. (1984). *Nouvelles Etudes sur l'Hystérie.* Paris: Joseph Clims.

Millot, C. (1983). *Horsexe. Essai sur le Transsexualisme.* Paris: Point Hors Ligne.

Perrier, F. (1978). Structure hystérique et dialogue analytique. In *La Chaussée d'Antin*, vol. 3. Paris: 10/18.

Perrier, F., and Granoff, W. (1979). Le problème de la perversion chez la femme et les idéaux féminins. In *Le Désir et le Féminin*. Paris: Aubier-Montaigne.

Porot, C. (1975). *Manuel Alphabétique de Psychiatrie*, 5th edition. Paris: PUF.

Stoller, R. J. (1975). *Sex and Gender: The Development of Masculinity and Femininity.* London: Karnac, 1994.

Tostain, R. (1978). Essai apologétique de la structure perverse. In *La Sexualité dans les Institutions.* Paris: Payot.

Index